JU JUTSU FUNDAMENTALS:
Terms and Techniques

By Launz Burch, San-dan
Samurai Ju Jitsu (Tasmania)
Australian Ju-Jitsu Association.

Ju Jutsu Fundamentals: Terms and Techniques

Cover artwork by Amy and April Underhill
Copyright © 2020 By Launz Burch
Published by: CAT Press

All rights reserved. No part of this publication may be reproduced, stored in a retrieval system, or transmitted in any form or by any means, by any person or entity (including Google, Amazon or similar organisations) without the prior permission in writing of the copyright holder concerned, nor be otherwise circulated in any form of binding or cover other than that in which it is published and without a similar condition, including this condition, being imposed on the subsequent purchaser.

A Cataloging-in-Publications entry for this title is available from the National Library of Australia.

ISBN-13: 978-0-6489917-1-7 (Trade Paperback)
ISBN-13: 978-0-6489917-0-0 (E-Book)

CAT Press
PO Box 3388, Darra
QLD 4076, Australia

Acknowledgements

I'd like to acknowledge the Australian Ju-Jitsu Association for their sterling work in promoting and supporting the art – and martial arts in general! – across this country. I would also like to acknowledge every instructor I've ever trained under, but that's quite a number by now, so I would particularly like to mention my first instructor Shihan Mark Haseman, who showed a skinny eighteen-year-old kid a great deal of kindness and patience. I'd also like to acknowledge the late and greatly missed Shihan Jan de Jong, who left an indelible impression on me with his patience, humour, kindness, and remarkably painful technique.

There are many more people who deserve acknowledgement for their help in bringing this volume to print, but I have space for only a few. My wife Natalie gave me time and space to pursue this passion of mine. Any number of friends have helped me over the years. The excellent Underhill sisters helped me turn this manuscript into a book. And of course, I absolutely must salute and thank my sister Aarjaun who is quite a martial artist in her own right, as well as being the publisher of this volume.

This book was written at the behest of my own students, who wanted access to a simple handbook of basic technique. I hope I've given them what they wanted in these pages, and I'd like to acknowledge newcomers and students in the art, wherever they are. You folk are the lifeblood of our tradition, and I hope this simple book helps you in the practice of this martial art, wherever you may be.

Table of Contents

A quick apologia	4
Introduction	5
Japanese pronunciation	6
Breathing and Kiai	8
Stances – *Tchi*	**11**
Forward leaning stance – *Zen kutsu dachi*	12
Back stance – *Kokutsu dachi*	13
Horseriding stance – *Kiba dachi*	14
Cat leg stance – *Neko ashi dachi*	15
Basic defensive posture – *Jigo hontai*	16
Falling techniques – *Ukemi waza*	**17**
Front fall – *Mae ukemi*	18
Side fall – *Yoko ukemi*	19
Forward shoulder roll – *Mae mawari ukemi*	20
Back fall – *Ushiro ukemi*	21
Throwing techniques – *Nage waza*	**22**
Leg throws – *Ashi waza*	24
Hip throws – *Koshi waza*	37
Sacrifice throws – *Sutemi waza*	47
Hand throws – *Te waza*	58
Joint locking techniques – *Kansetsu waza*	**72**
Standing joint lock techniques	75
Joint locking techniques as ground restraints	86
Joint lock techniques for ground-fighting	94
Striking and kicking techniques – *Atemi waza*	**102**
Kicking techniques	103
Hand striking techniques	112
Blocking techniques	**121**
Strangling and choking techniques – *Shime waza*	**131**
Hold-down techniques – *Osaekomi waza*	**141**
Anatomy and vulnerable points: making your technique count	151
The difference between learning the techniques and learning the art of Ju Jutsu	157
Further reading	158
Afterword	159
Basic terms and vocabulary	160

A quick apologia

This book started as a simple reference guide requested by some of my own students. They wanted a handy book that would help them remember Japanese names, and associate those names with techniques. Well – who was I to argue? I wouldn't have minded a book like that when I was starting out.

The first thing I did was check the Internet, of course. Turns out there's a whole lot of books on ju jutsu out there. But all of 'em I could find were tied to particular schools, teachers, styles, and systems. Or they were about competition and sport training. Or they were about hardcore self defense, or...

In the end I couldn't find a book that would act as a simple reference guide for students. I just wanted a book that presented a decent range of the more common basic techniques taught across various styles of ju jutsu. So – well, since I'm a writer as well as a ju jutsu instructor, I figured that if my students wanted a book like that, I might as well write one for them.

Here it is.

I've tried to keep it as simple as possible. I've stuck to basic, well-known, widespread foundational material. Each of the techniques is described as clearly and completely as I can figure out how to do it, and for most of them there's even a simple line-drawing illustration. Between the descriptions and the pictures, I think most students will be able to follow what's going on without too much trouble. It's not meant to be a teaching thing anyway. It's a tool to help people who already have an instructor and a dojo.

Those pictures, though... look, I'm a writer. And a martial artist. You didn't expect me to be Leonardo da Vinci as well, did you? I realise the art looks like *Bruce Lee Meets The Killer Potato Men* – but they'd look a whole lot worse if my colleague Sensei Amy Underhill hadn't put some polish over my own awful renderings. (Thank you, Sensei Amy!)

Next, let me acknowledge that here and there you may find a little of my sense of humour coming through. If you were expecting a whole lot of Zen and slightly pretentious philosophizing, you'll be disappointed. But I'll let you in on a secret: if you're going to keep training in any martial art, you'll need to find a way to have fun with it. And any system that can't survive a few laughs is probably an atrocious waste of time. I've been in and around ju jutsu for more than thirty years, and I'm happy to say that the people I've trained with have been some of the most relaxed, good-humoured, often hilariously funny individuals I've had the good fortune of meeting. If I'd tried to make this book a deadly serious thing, I expect some of those people would have come down to Tasmania just to point and laugh at me.

Finally, I'd like to thank a whole lot of people. I won't go naming them all, but I've trained under a decent number of different instructors across several different styles and systems, and I've learned from all of them. I'm also grateful to an impossibly long list of training partners and friends, and lately, grateful to people who train with me as 'students' now that I wear an instructor's belt. Everybody's given me something down the years, and if this book goes on to help anybody else, I'd like them to know it's a joint effort.

The only real martial arts lesson in this book: you can't learn a martial art by yourself!

Introduction

This book has been compiled as an aid to students of defensive-style and modern ju jutsu systems. It offers simple descriptions and information on a range of the basic techniques which are common to many of the different systems of ju jutsu.

In terms of technique, ju jutsu is an unusually broad art. Judo – an entire martial art based on throwing and grappling – was created in the late 19th century by Kano Jigoro from ju jutsu systems he had studied. Aikido – another entire martial system – was created in the first half of the 20th century by Ueshiba Morihei largely from his understanding of Daito-Ryu Aikijujutsu. Modern 'Brazilian jujitsu' is focused almost entirely on fighting on the ground – still another martial art built on the foundations of Japanese ju jutsu. Other arts which owe much of their existence to Japanese ju jutsu include Russian Sambo, and of course Krav Maga.

Japanese-style ju jutsu systems aren't limited to grappling, throwing, and groundwork. They include a wide variety of striking, kicking, and blocking methods and almost all incorporate kobudo, or 'lesser weapons' including short sticks, canes, staffs, and even chains and ropes.

It's a lot to learn.

The ideal of ju jutsu is that as you learn and practice techniques, you train your body to remember movements and patterns so that your responses come automatically, without planning. Eventually, all your training helps you abandon reliance on technique. You don't fight by imposing your techniques on the attacker. Instead, your opponent's attacks and tactics lead you to react instinctively, and the underlying principles of movement and balance, distance and angle, strike and evasion, trapping and unbalancing and so forth dictate your effective fighting responses.

That's an ideal. It's quite difficult to achieve. So you start by learning techniques. Dozens, scores, *hundreds* of techniques.

That's where this book comes in. It is not intended as an instructional text. You can't learn ju jutsu from a book. You need a teacher, you need a place to practice, and above all you need other people to learn with. A book is none of those things. This book is just a simple, low-level resource, offering Japanese names and translations, clear descriptions and images and notes. It can help you remember and understand various techniques, and help you avoid the more common errors.

This book is not a bible. There are many variations on every technique, and a large number of techniques aren't even included here. It's just a guide to a reasonable selection of basic techniques, introduced in the simplest possible manner.

Different instructors and different schools go about things in their own particular way. That is exactly as it should be. The term 'ju' doesn't just translate as 'gentle'. It also means 'flexible' or 'yielding', or even 'adapting'. No two people should practice ju jutsu in exactly the same way. Everyone is physically and mentally different, and different methods will work better for some, worse for others. **Where descriptions in this book differ from those provided by your school or instructor, you should follow your instructor's lead.** The basic principles of ju jutsu allow for techniques to be done in different ways depending on the needs of the situation.

I am not fluent in Japanese. While I recognise and respect the long history of Japanese ju jutsu, I think it's important to acknowledge it has become a world-wide art. Given that so many techniques of ju jutsu appear independently in other martial practices the world over, the value of learning Japanese terminology is perhaps not what it once was.

Nevertheless, most ju jutsu systems still use Japanese names for the techniques. This book attempts to follow that practice, but in the simplest manner possible.

All Japanese words are rendered in the English alphabet. Japanese personal names are supplied in the Japanese manner: family name, followed by individual name. In English we might speak of 'Jigoro Kano', but to the Japanese he is 'Kano Jigoro', and this book follows that protocol.

It is more difficult when it comes to names of techniques. For example, the 'major outer reap' is known worldwide. The English-alphabet version of the Japanese name is variously rendered as: O soto-gari; O soto gari; O-soto-gari; O sotogari, and even osotogari depending on which source you happen to encounter. In this book there will be no odd capital letters. Nor will there be too many dashes or hyphens. Correct or otherwise, the Japanese terms will be written as separate words: o soto gari.

The reasons for this separation are simple. First, given that no two sources seem to agree on how we should write Japanese words in English for martial arts, the simplest possible version is probably the best way to go. Secondly, if each martial technique name is broken into individual words, it will be easier for students to remember the terms and extend their knowledge. For example: *nukite* and *te-kubi* mean 'spear hand' and 'wrist'. But if you write them as *nuki te* and *te kubi*, and you realise that '*kubi*' translates as 'neck', then it is easy to see the connection between 'spear hand' and 'neck of the hand'. The word '*te*' for 'hand' becomes something the student can keep and recognise to help translate other terms.

In the body of the text, Japanese terms will be italicised to make them easily seen and recognised. The exceptions to this will be the words 'tori' and 'uke'. These very useful words will be kept as if adopted into English, because English has no convenient words that do the same job. In describing a martial technique (such as *o soto gari*) **tori is the person carrying out the technique**, and **uke is the person 'receiving' the technique**. In *o soto gari*, tori is the thrower and uke is the throwee. The words tori and uke will not be italicised because they're going to come up again and again, on almost every page.

Japanese pronunciation

I am by no means an expert on the topic of proper Japanese pronunciation, but if we're going to continue using Japanese terms in ju jutsu, it makes sense that we all pronounce them in much the same way so that people visiting from different dojos don't get confused. And of course, if we're going to try to pronounce the terms the same way, why not try to do it well enough that someone who speaks Japanese might actually understand us?

Here is a simple, basic guide to Japanese pronunciation. It's based on a semester of Japanese at university, and backed up with extensive reference to the Internet. It's almost certainly not perfect, but it's a good place to start.

1) *Pronounce every vowel.*
   In the English-alphabet version of the Japanese language, each syllable has a single vowel sound, and each vowel gets pronounced. There are no 'silent e' endings, for example. When you see two vowels together, they usually work as a diphthong – that is, you pronounce the first vowel and kind of slide into the second one to end. So the word *harai* (sweep) has two syllables: ha rai. The first is easy: 'hah'. The second is the diphthong, and should be pronounced 'ah-ee' without making the two sounds into two clear, distinct syllables.

2) *Actually, nothing is completely simple. The 'U' sound is the exception.*
   Much of the time, the 'U' isn't sounded unless it's at the end of a word. Thus ju jutsu is often written jiu jitsu because the Japanese don't give much value to that second 'u'. The pronunciation is closer

to "ju j'tsu" – which is how the English came to stick another 'i' in there instead of the 'u'.
This 'disappearing u' phenomenon even applies when the 'u' is the first vowel in what might be a diphthong. The word *sukui* (scoop, scooping) is therefore pronounced almost like 'ski'. If you listen really carefully to native Japanese speaker, you might hear a little hesitation, almost like a lengthening of the 's' in that 'ski' – but that's all the 'u' they'll give you.

3) *Every syllable ends in a vowel sound.*
That rule helps you break up words into syllables easily. There is an exception, of course: some syllables end in a soft 'n' sound or 'm' sound such as nihon (*ni* hon) or *tambo* (tam *bo*). Follow the spelling. You'll be okay.

4) *The vowel sounds don't change unless there's special punctuation to show it.*
Japanese vowel sounds are simple. Unlike English, there are no 'long' and 'short' vowels. The sounds they make are:
- A - 'ah'
- E - 'eh'
- I - 'ee'
- O - 'aw'
- U - 'ooh'

5) *Consonants are mostly reliable.*
There are no variable consonants in English-alphabet Japanese. G is always hard, as in 'good'. Y is always 'yuh', never 'ee'.

6) *Mostly, anyway.*
It's not that the consonants vary. It's that word pronunciation varies depending on where the consonant falls in some cases. Thus '*keri*' means 'kick'. But a front kick is not '*mae keri*', but '*mae geri*'. Just follow the spelling and you'll be okay.

7) *Japanese isn't as heavily accented as English.*
In English, we usually hit one syllable harder than the others, pronouncing it with more emphasis. (LOUder, in other words.) Japanese doesn't really do that. If you try to give every syllable of a word the same stress and length, you'll be about right. (It's a bit different over the length of a sentence – but we're using individual words, not full sentences. If you want conversational Japanese, get a different book.)

Putting all this together, you will readily see why I have chosen 'ju jutsu' as my own preferred spelling.
The Japanese use two characters for it in *kanji*, so it's most likely two words. The first 'u' in 'jutsu' is usually bitten off by native speakers, pronounced like a very short 'i' – but the word in *hiragana* (another way of writing Japanese) consists of two syllables: 'ju' and 'tsu'. There's no 'ji', so I won't be using it. And finally, I have no idea what the hyphen really represents so I'm leaving it out too. Ju jutsu.

But as usual: spell it however it suits you, your instructor, and your school. We're all talking about the same thing, no matter how we spell it.

Breathing and Kiai

It's hard to talk about the importance of breathing without sounding like an idiot. Everyone knows you have to breathe, right? Despite that, most people don't breathe efficiently, and in a situation as stressful as a violent confrontation, many people actually forget to breathe at all.

Breathing is the act of bringing fresh air into your lungs (inhaling) and pushing the used air back out (exhaling). In your lungs, the air comes into contact with specialized structures that permit your blood to pull oxygen out of the air, and dump carbon dioxide into it. Oxygen is the key: you need oxygen to generate energy in order to move and live. The more active your body becomes at any time, the more oxygen it requires to remain active. If you overexert yourself without breathing adequately, you'll find yourself collapsing and gasping, trying to draw more oxygen into your bloodstream to sustain yourself.

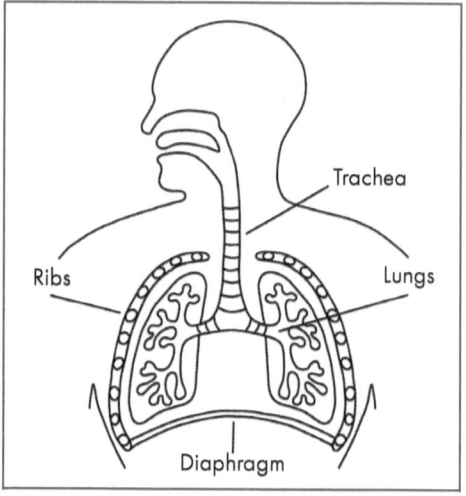

Unlikely as it sounds, there is an identifiable 'right way' to breathe. If you breathe properly, you maximise oxygen intake, and utilise abdominal muscles in ways that can enhance your ability to defend yourself. To understand this 'right way', it's useful to know how the physical act of breathing actually works.

Your lungs are rather like sponges surrounded by a protective cage of bone – the rib cage. The lungs have no muscle of their own, and the muscles between and around the ribs have only limited movement. Most of your ability to inhale and exhale comes from the broad, powerful band of muscle just below the lungs – the diaphragm. When you inhale correctly, the diaphragm moves downward into the body cavity, creating suction that draws air into the lungs. Correct breathing requires your abdominal muscles to relax so you can expand the body cavity and draw air in. You can test this for yourself: tighten your belly muscles as powerfully as you can, and try to draw in a deep breath. Go ahead. I'll wait.

Okay, that should do it. Didn't do you much good, did it? Now: consciously relax your belly muscles and breathe in. Imagine you're pulling air all the way down to your bellybutton.

Big difference, eh?

Breathing out is just the reverse. Tighten those belly muscles again, and this time consciously use them to force the air out of your lungs. Literally squeeze with your belly to push the air up and out.

Breathing is abdominal. When you breathe in, you must relax your abdominal muscles. When you breathe out, you must tighten those muscles and push the air out.

This really is no secret. Anyone who sings, or acts on the stage, or practices yoga, or swims competitively, or lifts weights, or any of a hundred other activities should be aware of this. Babies definitely understand it. Watch a baby breathe, and you'll see their belly lifts and drops with hardly any motion from the shoulders. That's because babies haven't yet been given a lifetime of bad postural and movement habits: they breathe properly because it's easy and efficient.

"Square Breathing" and the Navy SEALs

If conflict is stressful and can interfere with breathing, you'd imagine that people well trained for conflict would be aware of that, and would have a way of dealing with it. The US Navy SEALS are among the most highly regarded special forces in the world, and they're well known for what they call 'square breathing' or 'box breathing' as a means of reducing stress.

It's very simple. Settle yourself comfortably somewhere. Open your body up – don't hunch or compress your abdomen. Now, inhale strongly through the nose for four seconds, concentrating on pulling air down to your belly. Hold the air for four seconds. Exhale powerfully through the mouth for four seconds, squeezing your abdominals to empty your lungs. Hold on empty for four seconds – and then repeat the whole cycle.

This isn't a military secret. Essentially, the whole thing is borrowed from yoga. Who cares? It works. It oxygenates your blood, calms you, reduces stress – and if you do it at regular intervals for ten or twenty minutes at a time, it gets you into the habit of breathing correctly.

Breathing in action

When you're under stress, the first thing about breathing is to *remember to do it*. Trained pro fighters can have difficulty with this, so it's likely you will too. One way to do it is to train yourself to breathe whenever you take particular actions.

If you're simply waiting, observing, or moving, be aware of your breathing and try to keep to a pattern such as the 'square breathing' just mentioned. Your goal is to ensure you have enough oxygen to keep going – but not so much that you overload with oxygen (hyperventilate) and make yourself dizzy.

Some actions call for exhalation. Some call for inhalation. Remember: inhaling relaxes your abdomen, making you more flexible and potentially more vulnerable. Exhaling tightens the abdominals, allowing you to engage more of your core muscles to deliver power, and potentially helping you resist attacks to the abdomen.

Exhale powerfully when you strike. You'll notice that boxers do this. You can hear them hissing as they breathe past mouthguards, throwing punches. You may not be emptying your lungs completely with each strike – especially if you're throwing a series of strikes! – but the instant of tightening your abdominals and engaging your core will increase the power of your strikes, and will set up a pattern that reminds you to inhale as well as exhale.

Exhale when you are lifting or throwing your opponent. Again, the use of abdominal muscles will help engage your core, increasing your available muscular power and improving your body posture.

Exhale powerfully when receiving a strike, even if you're simply moving offline. If you misjudge and your opponent strikes your abdomen, it's good to be prepared to use those muscles to resist.

Definitely exhale when falling. Hitting the ground with lungs empty is much less painful and dangerous than hitting the ground with your lungs inflated. Think of a balloon: if you drop an inflated balloon it may well pop if it hits something sharp. Drop an empty balloon, and it comes to no harm.

With all this exhaling, you'll be wanting to know when to inhale. The answer is: whenever you need to, as long as you're not doing one of the actions already listed. Inhale as you rise to your feet from a fall. Inhale as you slip back to escape a strike. Inhale as you move behind your opponent, preparing to attack. Inhalation is less controlled, and offers no significant muscular or postural benefits – but you've gotta do it, or you'll pass out. Remember to control your inhalation, drawing air in with the belly muscles, through your nose. Try not to gasp and gulp for air: if your opponent is smart, they may realise you're struggling. They may even be smart enough to hit you in the belly while you're gulping for air. You don't want that.

Kiai and breathing

The old-school Japanese had a way of combining most of these ideas neatly, and adding a useful combative element in the process. *Kiai* translates roughly as 'spirit shout'. You will be most familiar with *kiai* from kung fu movies where the hero whines and shouts ferociously every time he strikes at an opponent. The famous 'hiyah!' of innumerable *karate* demonstrations is another well-known example.

Genuine, effective *kiai* is a powerful weapon as well as a means of directing and controlling your breathing in combat. Very simply: as you exhale sharply by tightening your belly muscles, use that exhalation to deliver the most powerful shout you can muster. The sound should be short, sharp, and overwhelmingly loud and penetrating.

The benefits to you are great. First, in a defensive situation making noise to attract attention is usually helpful. Second, remembering to breathe properly and use your abdominal muscles helps you make strikes more powerful. Third: a sudden, violent noise at close quarters is psychologically disruptive. If your *kiai* is strong, well-timed and unexpected, you may actually find your opponents 'freeze' for an instant – which is a huge advantage for you.

If you have the opportunity you can maximise the value of your *kiai* by keeping your voice low and calm before you actively engage. This has many benefits. If you're trying to defuse a situation, keeping a low, calm voice psychologically encourages others to be calm as well. And of course, if your *kiai* explodes violently into that apparent calm, it will seem all the more startling.

Using the opponent's breathing

Obviously, when you understand the basics of breathing you will see immediately that it provides opportunities for you in attack as well as defense.

Watch your opponent. If they are gasping and breathing heavily, they may be running low on oxygen and energy. Press the attack and make them exert themselves. The more oxygen demand you can force on them, the harder it will be for them to continue.

If they are panting regularly, try to time a strike for their inhalation. You are most likely to see this in their shoulders. (We may assume that if they're panting, they're not breathing properly – so look to the shoulders, not the belly.) Their shoulders will lift on inhalation, fall on exhalation. If you can hit them as they're beginning to inhale, their muscles will be relaxed and it will be difficult for them to muster strength to resist the strike.

If you are grappling, the time to attempt to throw or overbalance is as your opponent inhales. Also, watch for a particularly deep breath: many people will prepare for exertion by taking a deep breath, so this may signal that your opponent is about to try something.

If you are engaged on the ground, you can use your opponent's breathing to your advantage. Use your weight or your grip to compress their diaphragm. As they breathe out, increase the pressure as much as possible, and compress their body. If you can prevent them from being able to pull the diaphragm down into the body cavity properly, you can rapidly deoxygenate them and potentially even make them pass out.

Stances – *Tachi*

Forward leaning stance – *Zen kutsu dachi*	12
Back stance – *Kokutsu dachi*	13
Horseriding stance – *Kiba dachi*	14
Cat leg stance – *Neko ashi dachi*	15
Basic defensive posture – *Jigo hontai*	16

Stances are exactly what they sound like: particular standing postures used in training (and theoretically in conflict) to gain specific advantages of mobility, power, or stability. However, they are rarely used as 'stances'. That is, in actual use the ju jutsu practitioner hardly ever 'stands' in one spot, holding a posture. Combat is fluid. Mobility is paramount. If you stay still, your opponent will hit you.

This very simple truth makes the classic method of teaching 'stances' as static positions something of a problem. Certainly, to ensure that your body structure is strong and your balance is sound it's important to know where to put your feet, and how to support yourself. But learning those things without active movement – or worse, learning them with inappropriate movement – invites the student to think of stances as rigid, unchanging postures rather than what they are: brief moments in the course of a physical confrontation.

To help learn stances more effectively, it's useful to consider not just how the posture looks, but what it's intended to do, as well as what it does not do. For example: *kiba dachi* (horse riding stance) is wide and low. Quickly dropping into a side-on *kiba dachi* when your opponent has grabbed hold of you is an excellent way of strengthening your balance, dragging them off-balance, and making it difficult to throw you. On the other hand, *kiba dachi* is NOT a good stance from which to throw punches to the front. With your feet spread wide to either side, you have very little support in the front-to-back line so any punches you throw which make contact will tend to topple you back and destabilise you.

Understanding a stance allows for better practice. Standing in *kiba dachi* and throwing countless punches may strengthen your legs, but the action is actually conditioning you to respond (under stress, in conflict) in a way which is ineffective and possibly even dangerous. The habits we build in training by long repetition become the responses our bodies deliver when we have to react without thought. If we condition ourselves in training to throw straight punches from *kiba dachi*, we are likely to do exactly that in a fight. That's not a great idea, so it makes sense to train appropriate movements and stances together in a way which makes both stronger.

Hand position in the various stances is only marginally relevant. Good basic practices apply: keep the elbows close to your body and don't leave your hands hanging out in front of you after a strike or block. Your hands should be positioned where they're going to do you the most good in whatever conditions you happen to be using these stances. The karate practice of 'chambering' the fists to the hips before and after a strike is of questionable value in actual combat. In training, it teaches good finishing habits and ensures your straight-line strikes activate the right muscle groups, but in combat dropping your hands to your hips leaves your head and upper body exposed, and can act to telegraph your intent. It is perhaps better to concentrate on the body structure, foot position and balance when practicing stances, and leave the hands to do whatever job is most appropriate at the time.

Note that just like other techniques, there are variations in the way stances are taught and disagreements among different systems, styles and instructors as to how they should be performed and applied. As always, your own instructor and style should be your reference. This handbook is only an aid to memory, and the methods laid out here are open to discussion and examination.

Forward leaning stance – Zen kutsu dachi

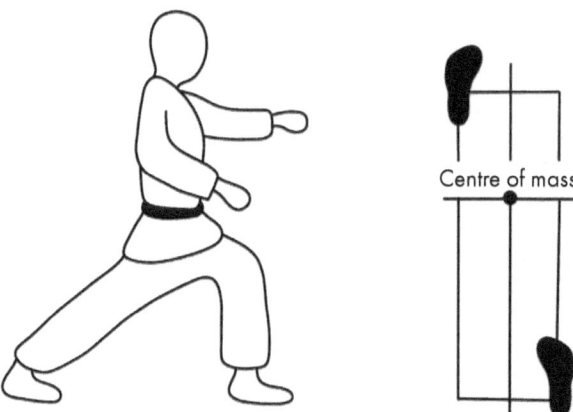

Description: Feet are slightly wider than shoulder width, equal distance from the centreline. The front leg is bent at the knee, so that the centre of gravity is lowered. The back leg is straight. Both feet point forward. The bend of the knee on the front leg is about 120 degrees. Back is straight, body and head upright, spine aligned. Ideally, if you glance down without moving your head you should just see the tip of your lead big toe sticking out in front of your knee.

Weight distribution: Approximately seventy percent of the body weight is on the front leg, the remainder supported by the back leg.

Uses: The resemblance to a fencer's lunge is telling. *Zen kutsu dachi* is a finishing position for a straight punch over the lead leg, or a reverse punch with the opposite arm. The body weight is driven forward and down by the deep step, allowing the body's momentum to add to the explosive power of the strike.

Variations: Some systems use a longer, lower version of this stance. Notably, many systems set the back foot at forty-five degrees off the centreline instead of forward. This angles the hips, while keeping the toes pointed forward squares the hips towards the target.

Notes:
- *Zen kutsu dachi* is strong and balanced along the front-back line, but is easily overbalanced to either side.
- The delivery of a long, lead-hand punch with this stance resembles the famous 'falling step' of the boxer Jack Dempsey, who was notable for the power of his strikes. Using a long step into this stance allows a reasonably fast and powerful long-range punch.
- The variation in stances may possibly be explained by the question of lead punches versus reverse punches. A reverse punch derives considerable power from 'snapping' the hip into the punch, which is delivered from the hand over the back leg. This squares the hips to face the opponent. A lead punch (*oi tsuki*) comes over the leading leg, and the arm extension tends to draw the shoulder and hip forward on that side. *Oi tsuki* is much more dependent on use of body weight and momentum than the reverse punch.
- *It is critical not to over extend on the front leg.* Your body weight must remain centred, not too far forward. If you overextend by bending the front knee too far, you stress the knee badly, weaken the strike, make yourself slow to recover balance and offer your opponent an opportunity to attack while you're overextended. Keep the back foot firmly planted and do not drag it forward with the strike.
- *Zen kutsu dachi* is the finishing stance for throws including *tai otoshi* and *kubi nage*.

Back stance – *Kokutsu dachi*

Centre of mass

Description: Heels are in line. Front foot points forward, back foot points out at ninety degrees. Back knee is bent, weight settled towards the rear of the stance. Front leg is also bent at the knee, but less sharply. Back is straight, head is held upright.

Weight distribution: Sixty to seventy percent of your weight is on the back leg, the remainder on the front.

Uses: The compressed back leg here acts like a spring. You fall back onto the leg to slip an attack, or to receive it with a trapping block. Then the back leg straightens and you can close distance quickly.

Variations: Some systems offset the back foot, placing the back heel outside the line of the front foot.

Notes:
- When using *kokutsu dachi* to receive a strike with a block of any sort, the front foot points directly towards the force of the attacker's blow.
- The front leg must remain bent at the knee. Straightening the front leg by sinking back and low just invites your opponent to stomp through your vulnerable, locked knee. Keeping the knee bent and keeping the front foot light enough to withdraw quickly allows you to protect the front leg from attack.
- *Kokutsu dachi* is strong on the front-to-back line. The turned back foot allows at least a little balance in the cross-line, but not much. Offsetting the back foot improves this, but at the cost of reducing the front-to-back strength of the stance.

Horseriding stance – *Kiba dachi*

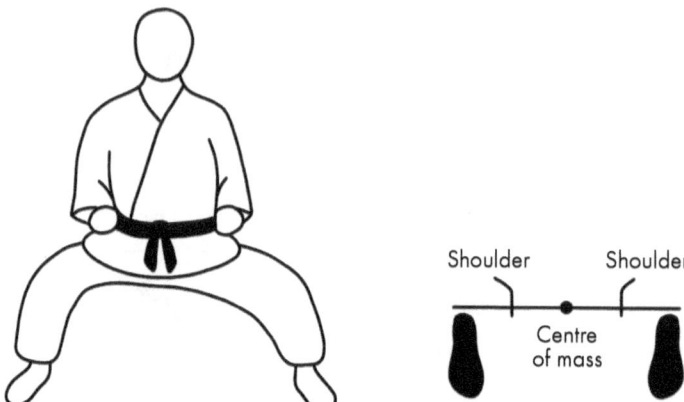

Description: Feet are placed wide to either side, facing forwards. Knees are bent and somewhat splayed outward, allowing the hips to settle low in the centre. Back is kept straight, head upright.

Weight distribution: Fifty-fifty between the two feet, with the main bodyweight centred low between the feet, directly over the line between the feet. There should be no sense of 'fighting' against falling backwards, but the body remains straight up and down, not leaning forward from the hips

Uses: *Kiba dachi* is a low, wide stance. It is used in the throw *kata guruma*. Because of its low centre of gravity it is also an excellent response to surprise grappling attacks. By stepping out to one side with one foot and allowing the bodyweight to lower in the centre you make it difficult for an opponent to pick you up or throw you. You also shift your body off their centreline, allowing you to strike more easily. *Kiba dachi* is also useful against grabs to clothes, wrists, etc. If you grip your opponent and turn side on to drop low into *kiba dachi*, your bodyweight will unbalance and destabilize your opponent, giving you the initiative while they attempt to recover.

Variations: Different systems advocate different widths for *kiba dachi*. It is easier to move out of a higher version of the stance, but lower versions offer more stability and resistance to grappling and throwing.

Notes:
- *Kiba dachi* is not a squat. The buttocks do not descend to the level of the knees or below.
- The stance is very stable from side to side, but has only limited strength in the front-to-back line. Any punches delivered to the front from this stance are just as likely to push you back as they are to harm your opponent.
- Side strikes, including *yoko geri*, *tetsui*, *uraken*, and even *shuto* can be delivered effectively from this stance.
- Weight is on the balls of the feet and the outer edges of the soles of the feet, not set back on the heels.

Cat leg stance – Neko ashi dachi

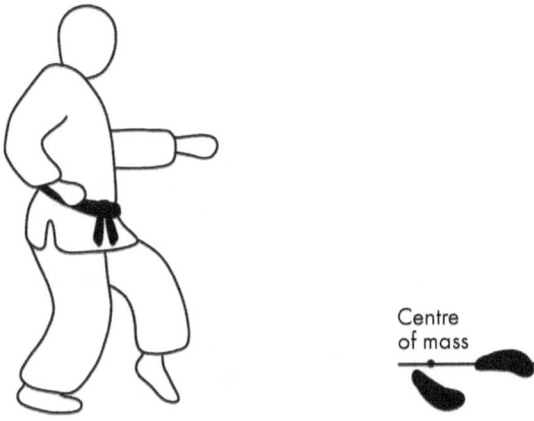

Description: Feet are in line, back foot angled, front foot facing forward. Both knees are bent, lowering the stance, but the front knee is bent in such a way that the ball of the foot only rests on the ground. Back is straight, head upright.

Weight distribution: Eighty to ninety percent of body weight rests on the back foot. The front foot is very light, able to move easily.

Uses: Neko ashi dachi is relatively high and unstable. It is used as a quick retreat – a slip back to evade an incoming kick or strike. The light front foot and bent back leg allow for quick movement in almost any direction. The front foot can even be used for quick, light kicks if needed.

Variations: Some styles bend the back knee even farther, for a deeper stance and therefore extend the front foot more. A deep stance that relies on one leg calls for a great deal of strength in that leg, and may potentially impede mobility.

Notes:
- Differentiated from *kokutsu dachi* in several ways. Feet are closer together and the front foot is lighter in *neko ashi dachi*, and the back foot is turned farther out in *kokutsu dachi*.

Basic defensive posture – *Jigo hontai*

Description: Knees somewhat bent. Feet a little wider than shoulder width, toes turned outwards a little more than usual. Two variants – *hidari jigotai* brings the left foot forward without changing the basic orientation of the feet, and *migi jigotai* brings the right foot forward similarly. Back straight, head upright.

Weight distribution: Fifty-fifty, with body weight centred between the feet. As always, weight is carried in the balls of the feet rather than the heels.

Uses: While the open, central, forward-facing *jigo hontai* is a little too vulnerable, both the left and right version are 'bladed', which is to say the hips face about forty-five degrees away from a potential attacker. These two stances are excellent, relaxed defensive postures which don't announce your training to an opponent. They allow for easy movement and quick attack or defense.

Variations: The judo version of this stance is a little lower and broader than many ju-jutsu versions. The higher stance is less obviously 'martial' or unnatural in appearance, and it still provides the benefits of quick movement, balance, and attack without sacrificing much in the way of stability.

Notes:
- *Jigo hontai* should be very little different from a simple, natural posture – just a little wider and lower.

Falling techniques – *Ukemi waza*

Front fall – *Mae ukemi*	18
Side fall – *Yoko ukemi*	19
Forward shoulder roll – *Mae mawari ukemi*	20
Back fall – *Ushiro ukemi*	21

Learning to minimise the danger of injury from a fall is a core skill in ju jutsu, and is taught across many martial arts. No matter how skilful you may be, physical conflict is always an uncertain space. Even the best can have a bad day, or just get plain unlucky. The idea that you're 'too good' to get taken to the ground is foolish. Learning break fall techniques is critically important, and practising them even more so.

Break falls – *ukemi waza* – aren't magic. They are the product of long testing and practice. The purpose of a break fall is to protect vital and/or easily damaged parts of the body by adjusting your fall so that the impact is taken by more robust or less critical parts. Generally, this means trying to redirect your fall so you land on parts like your flanks, particularly in the well-muscled (or well padded!) hip and shoulder areas.

Martial arts teach a range of falls, many of them quite spectacular when carried out enthusiastically. Please remember that falls which come off well in a training hall with a sprung floor and mats to help absorb the impact may not work so well in the uncertain environment of a real fight. As with every other aspect of ju jutsu training, you need to understand the principles at work, not simply replicate the techniques – and you need to practise.

For practice, you aren't limited to the training hall and the mats. If you're serious about making your ju jutsu work, you can – and should – train in more difficult conditions. Unlike the fighting techniques, the only person under threat is yourself so you can practice at will. It is worth knowing what it feels like to fall and roll on grass, on concrete, on gravel and dirt. It's also important to know just how much space you need to fall in, because not all fights occur in conveniently open spaces.

In general, falls to a hard surface work very similarly to falling on mats, but the usual judo-style 'slap' of the arm – designed to distribute impact across a padded surface, and to arrest a spinning fall from a throwing technique such as *tai otoshi* – is much less useful. When falling to a hard surface, you will rely more on good body posture, relaxation, and awareness of vital or easily damaged parts such as the head, ribs, wristbones, and the like. If you do choose to practice falling on hard surfaces, don't assume your familiarity with falling on a mat will make it easy. Start slowly, as if you were beginning all over again.

The truth is, falling onto concrete hurts. But if you learn to do it right, you won't break anything, and you'll get up again even if it hurts to do so.

Front fall – *Mae ukemi*

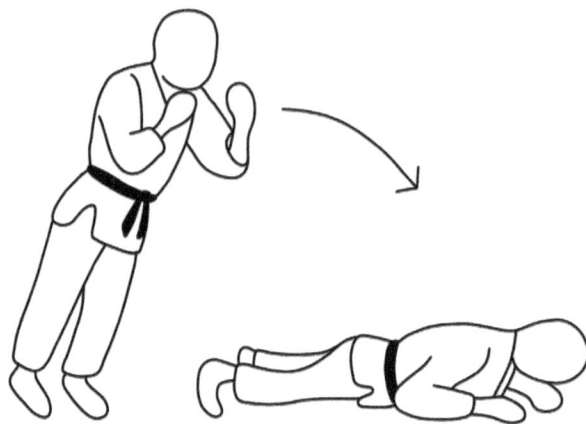

Description: From a standing position, raise your hands in front of you to collarbone level, palms forward, elbows splayed. Palms should be near central, in front of your chest. Allow yourself to topple forward. Before your body strikes the ground, slap sharply down with your palms and forearms. Strike firmly, and immediately stiffen the muscles of your arms and shoulders to accept the impact. When you hit, your palms should be roughly at the level of your face. Turn your face to the side as you hit in case of danger to the eyes from objects on the ground. Brace your body on the balls of your feet, forearms and palms protecting your groin and torso from impact – as if 'planking'. Torso, head and legs do not touch the ground.

Critical points: DO NOT extend or straighten your arms. Falling onto stiff arms is likely to fracture the smaller bones in your wrist. It is absolutely crucial that your arms are bent, to provide some 'spring' in the impact with the ground.

Uses: This is the fall you will use if your legs are taken from under you by something like a tackle from behind. It is also useful if your legs are trapped, and you cannot step forward or roll effectively.

Notes:
- This is a jarring fall inside a training hall with mats. On a hard, unforgiving surface it's downright bone-shaking. Done properly, however, it will protect you from serious harm. Broken wrists are the most common fractures seen by doctors – and the majority of them come as a result of falling onto a stiff, extended arm.
- When you're beginning with this fall, it's easier to learn it from a kneeling position. That lets you get the hand positioning right, and lets you get used to the fall. As you grow in confidence you can progress to a wide-legged stance, and then to a full-extension stance.

Side fall – *Yoko ukemi*

Description: (Right side – reverse for left) Bring your right arm up across your body from the shoulder. Put your weight on your left leg. Swing your right leg forward and across in front of you. Collapse your left leg so that you fall straight downwards, swinging your right leg clear. As your right hip hits the ground, your right arm swings back across. Continue to fall along the line of your right flank, slapping your right arm (palm downwards) on the mat just after your shoulder strikes the mat. Your right leg should be fully extended. Your left leg should be bent at the knee and cocked, left foot flat on the floor behind your right calf, and you should be lying on your right side.

Critical points: Always fall to the side of the extended leg. Always collapse the other leg so you fall straight down to your hip, rather than toppling. Remember to keep your head raised, and your teeth closed. Remember that your right arm strikes the ground parallel to your right leg, not raised up towards your head.

Uses: This is probably the most versatile of the break fall techniques. With this, you can fall without harm within an arc of approximately 270 degrees, excluding only the 90 degree window directly in front of you. If you are falling to a hard surface, you are better off to fold your arm across your chest to ensure you land on your shoulder rather than slapping at the ground.

Notes:
- The key is falling along the line of your flank. Your body should reach the ground in this order: right ankle, right outer calf, right thigh, right hip, right side and shoulder, and finally right arm and hand.
- When you fall on the mat and use your arm to slap, the slapping arm should end up parallel to the extended leg, and both should be angled about 45 degrees from the line of the body.

Forward shoulder roll – *Mae mawari ukemi*

Description: (Left side – reverse for right.) Step forward with the left foot and reach forward towards your centerline with the left hand. Turn the left hand palm downward, thumb pointing to the space between your feet. Bend your left knee and push off from your right foot, allowing your body to topple forward over your left leg. Tuck your head in. As your left palm strikes the mat, round your arm so that the contact with the mat moves from hand to fore-arm to upper arm to shoulder. If your head is properly tucked in and you have pushed off firmly from your right foot, your legs will be extended and you will be rolling forward. Let the momentum of your legs carry your lower body over and past. Mat contact will move from left shoulder to right hip. At this point, tuck your feet in and allow your forward momentum to carry you smoothly back to a standing position.

Critical points: This fall must be done over the same shoulder as the leading leg. Trying to roll over the other shoulder will square you up and force a true somersault, placing your spine in prolonged contact with the ground.

Uses: *Mae mawari ukemi* is a core falling technique in judo and ju jutsu. Mastery of this fall allows you to practice many of the more interesting and dangerous throws safely. It is also very useful if you simply happen to stumble and fall in the outside world – although of course, it requires space. *Mae mawari ukemi* can also be used for diving over obstacles, which can be handy.

Notes:
- If you have difficulties with this fall initially, try doing it from a kneeling posture. Raise the lead knee. Position the lead hand exactly as described before. Push off from the back foot strongly, bring your lead hand down in front as you go over, tuck your head and you will roll through neatly.
- The purpose of this roll is to protect your spine and your neck. A classic somersault compresses the neck and brings the spine into contact with the ground. Properly carried out, *mae mawari ukemi* distributes the pressure of contact along the arm, the shoulder, the hip and the leg. It is far less stressful to your body.

Back fall – Ushiro ukemi

Description: Widen your stance until your feet are slightly more than shoulder width apart. Bend your knees and lean into a half-crouch, bringing your arms in front of you. Allow your knees to collapse smoothly so your body moves straight down, your head still centred and upright. As you pass the point of balance, your body will naturally fall backwards. Tuck your head and curve your spine. As your buttocks touch the mat, allow yourself to roll back, bringing your feet up in front of you. Your arm now spread out so that you slap the mat, palms down, with your arms at roughly 45 degrees from your body on either side. If you desire, you may raise your feet and use their weight as a counterbalance to let you roll back up to stance.

Critical points: Remember to collapse your knees. Don't fall backwards like a tree.

Uses: Very handy on the mat, but less useful outside. This fall brings you straight back along your spine. If there's anything on the ground in your way, it's going to hurt. For a safer fall, you are far better off turning your body as you go so that you land along your hip and shoulder in *yoko ukemi*.

Notes: This fall becomes a back roll very easily. At the point where you're on your back with your feet raised, turn your head to the right, and use your momentum and your core muscles to throw your feet over your right shoulder. If you put sufficient energy into the movement, your feet will carry your body past the point of balance and you will roll smoothly over your right shoulder to a crouching position. Obviously, you can perform the same movement over the left shoulder if you desire – but remember to turn your head to face left first. The turn of the head prevents you twisting your spine as you go through the roll.

Throwing techniques – Nage waza

Leg throws – *Ashi waza*	**24**
Leg wheel – *Ashi guruma*	25
Advancing foot sweep – *De ashi barai*	26
Lift-pull foot sweep – *Harai tsurikomi ashi*	27
Knee wheel – *Hiza guruma*	28
Minor outer reap – *Ko soto gari*	29
Minor inner reap – *Ko uchi gari*	30
Major outer reap – *O soto gari*	31
Major outer wheel – *O soto guruma*	32
Major inner reap – *O uchi gari*	33
Sliding leg sweep – *Okuri ashi harai*	34
Propping and drawing ankle throw – *Sasae tsurikomi ashi*	35
Inner thigh throw – *Uchi mata*	36
Hip throws – *Koshi waza*	**37**
Major hip throw – *O goshi*	38
Floating hip throw – *Uki goshi*	39
Rear hip throw – *Ushiro goshi*	40
Hip wheel – *Koshi guruma*	41
Sweeping hip – *Harai goshi*	42
Sleeve lift and pull hip – *Sode tsurikomi goshi*	43
Lifting and pulling hip throw – *Tsurikomi goshi*	44
Spring hip – *Hane goshi*	45
Changing hip throw – *Utsuri goshi*	46
Sacrifice throws – *Sutemi waza*	**47**
Crab claw (scissors) throw – *Kani basami*	48
Outer winding throw – *Soto makikomi*	49
Circular throw – *Tomoe nage*	50
Corner throw – *Sumi gaeshi*	51
Valley drop – *Tani otoshi*	52
Rear throw – *Ura nage*	53
Side drop – *Yoko gake*	54
Side wheel – *Yoko guruma*	55
Side separation – *Yoko wakare*	56
Rice bag reversal – *Tawara gaeshi*	57
Hand throws – *Te waza*	**58**
One arm shoulder throw – *Ippon seoi nage*	59
Two arm shoulder throw – *Morote seoi nage*	60
Shoulder wheel – *Kata guruma*	61
Neck throw – *Kubi nage*	62
Scooping throw – *Sukui nage*	63
Body drop – *Tai otoshi*	64
Floating drop – *Uki otoshi*	65
Two-handed reap – *Morote gari*	66
Dead tree drop – *Kuchiki taoshi*	67
Four direction throw – *Shiho nage*	68
Head turning throw – *Hachi mawashi*	69
Entering throw – *Irimi nage*	70
Back-bending throw	71

All systems of ju jutsu incorporate techniques of overthrowing the opponent, but methods of throwing are commonplace in martial arts around the world. Early English wrestling manuals show illustrations which look very much like the modern 'hip throw'. Ancient Greek vases show images of men using leg trips and sweeps as they try to unbalance one another.

The throws listed here are all well-known, and commonly taught. They are broken into subsections as dictated by Judo (which was itself created from ju jutsu by Kano Jigoro in the 19th century) for ease of memory and identification. Not all the throws listed here are still legal in judo competition, but ju jutsu is the older art and many ju jutsu systems retain brutal and dangerous techniques which Kano deliberately left out of his "gentle way".

The use of a judo framework is deliberate. The old, brutal ju jutsu throws frequently include strikes and dangerous joint-locking techniques. Kano's system, which "softened" the approach to allow judo to become a competitive sport, makes throwing relatively safe for newcomers to the art. Once the basic principles of a throw are properly understood, an advanced student can add in elements such as striking and joint-locking, confident that they can look after their training partner in the process.

Used in self-defense, throwing techniques are powerful. Untrained people don't know how to fall properly, and when they are slammed to the ground it takes them some time to get back up – if they get up at all. It's important to exercise control when practising throws. You want your training partners to keep working with you, and you don't want to inadvertently kill someone even in self-defense.

Throwing techniques are usually described in three parts: *kuzushi*, where tori breaks uke's balance and sets uke in motion; *tsukuri* or 'entry', where tori takes the proper physical position and place; and *kake*, or the execution of the throw. In judo, the *kuzushi* is usually achieved by pushing or pulling uke, or by responding to uke's movement. In practical ju jutsu, *kuzushi* frequently comes from the momentum of uke's attack. When this isn't appropriate, practical ju jutsu throws often come from sharp, disruptive strikes designed to do what the pushes or pulls of judo do. In more brutal cases, a ju jutsu practitioner will use a joint-locking technique to drive uke into the throw. Nevertheless, for safety of learning and training the judo push-pull system of breaking balance is an effective starting place, and the throws listed here are described in that fashion.

For ease of description – and simply because it also the most common method by which these throws are taught – the throws are depicted from a simple, *standard judo grip*. The standard judo grip requires that both players have a *gi* jacket. The left hand holds the partner's right sleeve at the elbow. The right hand takes a strong grip on the partner's left lapel. Though the hands hold strongly, the arms are usually relaxed. This grip is not mandatory in competition, and players will shift their grip to suit themselves as they attempt to throw one another – but for purposes of learning throws, this is the hold which is most often used.

Each of the throws listed here includes a simple image and a description, which will provide handy guidance. Also included are quick notes on the 'defensive value' of the throws. This refers to how useful each of the throws is likely to be in an actual confrontation. Not all throws are equally useful. Some have very particular applications or purposes, and some seem especially suited for sporting competition over actual defense.

Each throw also lists a number of 'counters' and 'combinations'. Counters are throwing techniques used to counter an attempted throw; that is, they are defensive responses to a 'throw' attack. The act of trying to throw uke places tori in a particular, predictable position for each different throw. If uke is quick and perceptive enough, uke can shift to take advantage of that, and successfully throw tori instead.

Combinations are 'follow-up' throws which take advantage of the most common escapes. Tori attempts a throw. Uke evades the throw in a predictable fashion, and if tori is quick and perceptive, tori can use uke's movement and position to set up for a second throw. The use of combinations and counters is embedded in *randori*, the competitive grappling of judo. More importantly, these techniques promote a mindset of flexibility and adaptability – the core of ju jutsu itself.

Leg throws – Ashi waza

These throws are grouped together because the finishing action is dependent on the work of legs and feet in particular. The Leg Throws include some of the simplest, most practical, and best known of the throws. Because they depend strongly on actions like sweeping and tripping, these throws are also fairly easy to adapt to a non-sporting situation, where your opponent may not be wearing a nice, convenient jacket.

One thing to note about Leg Throws: being tall and/or long-legged is a real advantage. You have more reach and more mobility. It is easier for a tall, long-legged opponent to step around or otherwise avoid leg throws from a shorter opponent. Conversely, it's difficult for a shorter opponent to evade the reach and power of leg throws from a taller partner.

Leg wheel – Ashi guruma

Description: With the left foot positioned near or in front of uke's left foot, tori pulls upward on uke's collar and pivots sharply to the left. Drawing uke's lead arm across tori's body, tori pulls uke into the pivoting action and sweeps powerfully back with the right leg at shin level. Tori continues to pull uke in winding fashion, like turning a wheel with both hands, while completing the sweep.

Common problems: If tori's left foot is too central, or even close to uke's right there will be difficulty lifting the collar and breaking uke's balance. Tori must remember to 'wheel' with the hands as they pull uke through, not simply drag uke into the sweep by main strength.

Defensive value: Effective against a pushing attack. Useful against a haymaker if tori slips inside the striking arc of the attacker and takes control of the attacker's right hand and left shoulder. Strong throw, difficult to escape once it's in action. Both feet leave the ground in this throw and the fall is jarring.

Counters: Uke can pull back against tori's *kuzushi*, and attack tori's right foot for *de ashi harai* as tori attempts the sweep. *Ko soto gake* and *ko soto gari* can also be used this way. Uke can also widen their stance, drop their weight and attempt *ushiro goshi*.

Combinations: If uke steps around with the right leg, tori can adjust position and attack uke's left inner thigh with a powerful sweep for *uchi mata*. Alternately, tori can pull to increase uke's motion and pivot into *morote seoi nage*.

Notes:
- Sweeping both uke's legs makes the fall heavy and jarring. Good for defense.
- This throw becomes more powerful if tori uses their right arm to underhook uke's left, and drive up through the armpit as tori turns for the throw.
- Retain uke's left arm during the fall to move quickly into an arm bar for control on the ground.

Advancing foot sweep – De ashi barai

Description: Tori draws uke forward with their left hand by pulling uke's right sleeve forward, down, and left. As uke steps onto their right foot to compensate, tori uses their left instep to sweep uke's right ankle across uke's body. Tori completes the throw by pulling sharply down and left on uke's sleeve, and pushing on uke's left shoulder with their right hand.

Common problems: Tori should use their handgrips to draw uke to the left, and sweep the foot in the opposite direction. Pulling the foot forward can allow uke to land their weight and find balance. Pushing backward actually supports uke, helping uke escape the fall. Timing is crucial for this throw – the foot sweep should occur at the moment uke's balance is coming forward and their right foot is about to land. An earlier attack may allow uke to escape by shifting balance to their left foot, while a late attack may allow uke to plant their right foot before it can be swept.

Defensive value: Can be used against an advancing threat, but isn't much use in the fight unless uke throws a committed strike over the lead foot, and tori is very quick and precise. Best used during pushing and shoving before uke starts striking in earnest.

Counters:
- If uke can transfer balance to the left foot in time and leave the right foot light, uke can circle their right foot around tori's sweep and counter with a sweep of their own, pulling tori to the right into *de ashi barai*.
- Uke can skip inward with the left foot, closing the gap and allowing them to counter with *o uchi gari* using the right leg.

Combinations:
- If uke defends by planting their weight on the right leg, tori, can slip behind for *sukui nage*.
- If uke withdraws the right leg, tori can change direction and attack with a right-leg *o uchi gari*.

Notes:
- Timing and precision are critical with this throw.
- If tori has strong control over uke's right arm, they can slow uke's step and drive uke to the side, giving more time for the foot sweep.

Lift-pull foot sweep – *Harai tsurikomi ashi*

Description: Tori advances on uke, who walks backward. As uke prepares to shift their weight to the right foot, tori takes a deep stride to close the gap and attacks uke's right ankle with a left-foot sweep that pushes the foot back. At the same time, tori lifts uke sharply and uses their handgrip to pull uke up, back, and to the left.

Common problems: The timing of the *kuzushi* and the foot sweep are crucial. Tori must commit strongly to the *kuzushi* while simultaneously carrying out the footsweep – and both these actions must occur just as uke commits to shifting their weight, and before that shift is complete. Failure with any of these component actions will probably result in failure of the throw.

Defensive value: This throw is strongly dependent on the jacket grip. It also ignores one of the primary principles of ju jutsu – the *kuzushi* is upwards and forwards to uke, but uke is moving backwards and lowering their weight while this is supposed to happen. Most throws utilize uke's momentum and movement. This one actively opposes those things. As a genuine piece of self-defense, *harai tsurikomi ashi* has limited value.

Counters:
- Uke can turn to their right, withdrawing the right foot and pulling tori onto their left foot, allowing uke to attack with a left foot *ko uchi gari*.
- Uke can slip the footsweep, lean into tori's *kuzushi* and execute a right-foot *o uchi gari*.

Combinations:
- If uke yields to the *kuzushi* and slips the footsweep, tori can lower their grip and attempt *ura nage*.
- If uke resists the *kuzushi* with strength and lowers their balance, tori can slip in quickly for *kuchiki taoshi*.

Notes:
- This is a relatively low-percentage throw compared with near-twin *sasae tsurikomi ashi*, which is carried out with uke going forward and tori going backwards.

Knee wheel – Hiza guruma

Description: With uke's left leg forward, tori pulls sharply with their left hand and presses uke's right knee with their left foot, blocking the knee from moving forward. Tori uses the foot press to prevent uke's attempt to step forward and regain balance. Tori completes the throw by pulling uke over to the left, using both hands in a 'wheel' action that should draw uke over the blocked knee.

Common problems: Tori's pull must be correctly aligned at right angles to uke's baseline. Pulling uke towards tori's body will not effectively break uke's balance.

Defensive uses: Hiza guruma can be done with an arm grip and a strike to the head or neck for unbalancing. It is also possible to kick or push through uke's knee from the side to collapse the leg and make breaking balance easier. Although less technically correct (reduced 'guruma' or wheel action) this is a powerful defensive throw in the right circumstances.

Counters:
- Uke can shift the left-hand grip to the collar, grab tori's belt with the right hand, and drop into yoko guruma.
- Uke can go wide around tori's attacking foot and move to a deep *kiba dachi* to pull tori into an *uki otoshi*.
- Uke can turn inwards (left), draw down on tori's right arm and attempt o soto gari.

Combinations:
- If uke withdraws the right leg successfully and turns their body to the right to resist the *kuzushi*, tori can change the direction of the *kuzushi* and attack with a left-foot o uchi gari.
- If uke steps wide around the attacking foot, tori can shift direction and attack with *ko soto gari* or *ko soto gake* using the right leg.

Notes:
- The option of kicking through the knee joint from the side angle to collapse it is dangerous and should be reserved for serious self-defense situations.
- The kick or push through the knee option allows this to be used effectively when uke is forward on the leg, making the throw versatile in self defense.

Minor outer reap – Ko soto gari

Description: Tori presses forward, pushing uke with their right hand, pulling down on uke's sleeve with their left, and attacking uke's lead right foot in a sweep with their left. The sweep traps uke's foot bringing it up and across tori's body. Tori completes the throw by pushing uke's left shoulder away and drawing back and down on uke's right arm.

Common problems: Tori needs to move around towards uke's right during the attack. This throw doesn't take uke straight backwards, and attempting to do that may allow uke to recover balance. The throw is to uke's back right corner.

Defensive value: Ko soto gari is a quick, simple trip. It's easily done even without a heavy jacket to rely on. Right hand can unbalance with a strike to the side of the head, or even drive through the throat. Left hand needs only to guide uke's right elbow, trapping it in close as tori drives forward. This is a useful throw in a standing clinch or grappling situation. Particularly effective if uke has reached for collar control, planning to throw a punch with the other hand as tori can defend against the possible strike by raising their right arm into position to carry out the throw.

Counters:
- Uke can drive in strongly and attempt a right-leg o uchi gari.
- Uke can slip the sweep, underhook tori's left with their right arm and pivot for a strong ashi guruma.

Combinations:
- If uke slips back with the right leg, tori can change direction and attempt a left-leg ko uchi gari.
- Alternately, tori can step through with the right foot and pivot into seoi nage.

Notes:
- Similar to – often indistinguishable from! – ko soto gake, or minor outer hook. In ko soto gake, tori usually traps the swept leg close to themselves and drives more towards uke's rear, rather than their back right corner where ko soto gari goes.
- Also quite similar to de ashi harai, but doesn't rely on uke trying to step forward into the throw.

Minor inner reap – *Ko uchi gari*

Description: Tori angles themself right-side towards uke. Controlling uke's upper left quarter with their right arm, tori drives forward and left with the right shoulder while trapping uke's right foot behind the heel with their own right foot. As tori pushes with the right shoulder, their right foot sweeps back towards their left, pulling uke's foot with it, forcing uke into the fall.

Common problems: The attacking shoulder and sweeping foot should happen at the same time. Leading with either one gives uke an option for escape. The throw must be made with full commitment, or uke may successfully resist. The attacking push must bring uke over their right foot. If the attack is too straight-line, uke may be able to keep their weight on their left foot and lift the right to escape the sweep.

Defensive value: Effective on the inside line against pushes or right-hand attacks. The drive with the shoulder can be replaced with a thrusting palm against the left side of uke's face, driving the head back and over the right foot. Can also be done from a close clinch.

Counters:
- Uke can turn sharply to the left, transfer weight to the left foot and counter with *ko uchi gari* by driving at tori with their right shoulder.
- Uke can pivot sharply to the left 270 degrees, retaining the right arm to put tori in position for *seoi nage*.

Combinations:
- If uke escapes by withdrawing the right foot, tori can quickly hook their right foot behind uke's left and push uke in that direction, setting up for *o uchi gari*.
- If uke resists by pushing tori back, tori can turn quickly left 90 degrees for *seoi nage*.

Notes:
- *Ko uchi gari* commits tori to a forward motion and engages tori's forward leg. This often leads to tori falling with uke, albeit in a strong upper position. Care should be taken if the throw is used in self-defense.

Major outer reap – O soto gari

Description: Controlling uke's right arm, shoulder and head, tori pushes uke's upper body back and steps deep with the left leg. Tori's right leg then swings through the gap and drives back, sweeping uke's right leg. Tori completes the throw by using the upper body control to push uke down and left in opposition to the sweep of the leg.

Common problems: If tori does not break uke's balance by controlling and driving uke's upper body back, uke can easily push back and counter the throw by using the same technique against tori. The *kuzushi* is critical in this throw.

Defensive value: Good against 'round' or 'hook' attacks over an advancing leg. Tori should defend strongly into the attack to power the *kuzushi* and set up the leg sweep. Head and upper body control can be achieved with palm strikes to the face or grips to the throat, or simply a right arm across the neck.

Counters:
- Counter with *o soto gari* by pushing in, or turning to break tori's balance so you can perform the sweep instead of them.
- Counter with *seoi nage* by gripping tori's left arm and turning quickly ahead of them so they fall forward onto your back for the throw.

Combinations:
- If uke pushes back, grip their left arm and turn quickly around so they fall onto your back for *seoi nage*.
- If they successfully withdraw their right foot, push in and across with your right foot to attack their left leg for *o uchi* gari, while drawing their upper body to your right and away from you.

Notes:
- The most common attack thrown in fistfights is a right haymaker. This attack occurs with the left foot advanced. *O soto gari* can be used, but it should be the left-hand version which attacks the lead left leg instead of the right leg.
- Against straight or overhead attacks, you can slip the attacker's right arm and control their balance with your own right arm across the attacker's neck and left collarbone. This places you outside the attacker's right arm, and helps prevent any follow-up attacks from the left hand while still maintaining control over the right shoulder and upper body.

Major outer wheel – O soto guruma

Description: Similar to o soto gari, tori drives uke back and to uke's right by controlling the uke's upper body and right arm/shoulder. Tori steps past on the left leg, and extends the right leg firmly across the back of uke's legs, right ankle at about the level of uke's right knee. Keeping the leg strongly in place, tori drives with the right shoulder and pulls down and around with the left arm, causing uke to 'wheel' over the axis created by tori's right leg.

Common problems: Performing a textbook o soto guruma is challenging, as tori is not really supposed to sweep with the right leg, but simply extend it powerfully so that uke falls over it.

Defensive value: The fall is harder than o soto gari, and more jarring for uke. Otherwise, this throw is on a par with o soto gari for defensive use.

Combinations and counters: See o soto gari

Notes:
- Judo makes distinctions between throws based on the perceived principle of the throw. This throw is a 'guruma' or 'wheel' because tori's leg acts as a block, and uke is 'wheeled' over it by the thrust of tori's hands and shoulder. Despite that, judo still classifies this as a 'leg throw'.
- Understanding the 'wheel' principle is useful and valuable. But for practical purposes if tori sweeps with the leg as well as using hands and shoulder, the throw is just as effective – in fact, rather more so.
- Another variation here is o soto otoshi, or greater outer drop. In this case, tori's right leg slides down the back of uke's right leg with a stomping action, and tori turns their *kuzushi* more to tori's left, throwing uke in a more sideways direction over the leg.
- O soto gari, o soto guruma and o soto otoshi all bear a similarity to the most basic form of *irimi nage*. *Irimi nage* does not use the leg at all, instead relying on entering deeply to offbalance uke, and on using the right arm to turn uke across their back left corner into the weak point of their stance created by advancing the right leg.

Major inner reap – O uchi gari

Description: Tori pushes uke's right shoulder back to lighten uke's balance on their left leg, and moves in to hook tori's right leg around uke's lower left leg. Continuing to push uke back and to tori's right, tori hooks uke's leg powerfully up and behind, forcing uke to fall to their back left corner.

Common problems: If tori drives uke straight back instead of including the drive to tori's right, uke may be able to rebalance. If tori hooks uke's leg out to tori's right instead of entangling it and ensuring it rises up behind tori, uke may be able to maintain posture on their other leg.

Defensive Uses: Tori can reach across uke's throat with their right fore-arm and elbow to push uke back and to the right, allowing this throw to work without a jacket. Maintaining a grip on uke's elbow is still valuable, but tori can strike with the right hand rather than pushing. If the strike is well timed with the leg sweep, the throw is sharp, abrupt and effective. If executed promptly it can be a good answer to the common 'right haymaker', thrown by uke with the right foot held back.

Counters:
- If uke can slip the sweep, uke can pivot to their left and underhook tori's left arm, allowing a strong *ashi guruma*.
- A sharp left pivot from uke combined with underhooking tori's right arm with uke's right arm puts uke in position to attempt *seoi nage*.

Combinations:
- If uke slips the sweep by withdrawing the left foot, tori can change their angle and attack uke's right foot from the inside with *ko uchi gari*.
- Tori could also release the right hand-grip, draw uke sharply to tori's left and downward, and attack with a left-foot *de ashi harai*.

Notes:
- When tori maintains their grip on uke during the sweep, it is very common for both tori and uke to fall. Tori falls in a superior position, but this still isn't ideal in defense, although it's less troublesome in sport competition. The attacking version with no left hand grip from tori and tori's right hand gripping uke's right collar and using the right forearm to drive against uke's throat makes it easier for tori to maintain balance and control.

Sliding leg sweep – *Okuri ashi harai*

Description: Using the standard judo grip, tori and uke move sideways in parallel with a synchronized skipping motion. As uke rises up in the middle of a skip, tori moves ahead with their leading leg and drives upward with their grip. Tori sweeps strongly with their trailing leg, catching both of uke's legs and lifting them upwards in the direction the pair were skipping. As the sweep happens, tori pulls in the direction opposite the skipping, and downward. As uke falls, tori releases the grip of the leading hand and holds uke's sleeve with the trailing hand so uke's body can rotate in the air and land safely.

Common problems: Missing the timing on the skip-step will result in tori kicking uke painfully in the ankle without achieving a throw. Uke needs to be at the height of their skip, and it's important for tori to drive upward to make the sweep easier. Also, discerning any reason ever to use this throw is quite a challenge.

Defensive uses: Should you find yourself threatened during a foxtrot, or perhaps a spirited waltz, this throw is particularly handy. You may find that acquiring a solid grip on a strapless ballgown is challenging. Retain the elbow grip and simply strike the side of your partner's head with your other hand to drive their upper body in the direction you need them to go. Once your dance partner has been hurled to the floor, it is advisable to leave the ball swiftly. It is unlikely that the hosts will understand why you have found it necessary to take violent action, and it's best to exit before unpleasant questions are asked.

Counters: Instead of skipping sideways uke can drive forward strongly into *o soto gari*. Or perhaps slip the grip and shoot for *morote gari*. Or perhaps simply refuse any further dance requests, since tori is obviously a graceless oaf with two left feet. What is he even doing on the dance floor?

Combinations: Depending on the music, tori may decide to change from waltz to salsa, or possibly even a mazurka if the conditions require it. Not a tango, however. That way lies madness.

Notes:
- Yes. It's hard to take this throw seriously. But if you do find yourself in a close grip, you can try driving upwards and to the side, and sweeping the feet in the opposite direction – which is more or less *okuri ashi harai*, but without all the sliding and skipping.
- Should you ever find yourself skipping sideways in time with your mortal enemy, take a moment to consider your life choices.
- There's probably a use for this throw. Somewhere. Somehow. Anyway, it's commonly taught and it does embody some useful principles.

Propping and drawing ankle throw – Sasae tsurikomi ashi

Description: Tori shifts their right foot to the right, outside uke's stance. Pulling uke strongly leftwards and towards tori's back corner, tori props their left instep against uke's right ankle, preventing uke from moving the foot forward. Tori completes the throw by continuing to pull uke past tori's left side, back and down.

Common problems: Tori must step offline before attempting the throw.

Defensive value: This is an excellent defensive throw if you're being pushed back. Shifting off-line and propping the left ankle leaves uke overbalanced and easily pulled into the throw.

Counters:
- If uke can slip the ankle prop, tori is open for a strong o uchi gari.
- Stepping around the ankle-prop also offers uke the opportunity to enter for ushiro goshi.

Combinations:
- As uke attempts to step around the ankle prop, tori can change direction of the kuzushi and drive for left-foot ko uchi gari.
- Tori can also turn sharply right as uke steps around the prop, and use tori's already-extended left leg for ashi guruma.

Notes:
- Some judo sources suggest that the propped ankle should already be set and weight-bearing, so that tori drags uke over and past the point of balance. Others suggest that the ankle-prop should occur early, before uke's weight is set allowing tori to trip uke easily with the throw. Whichever is doctrinally correct, it's easier to prop early and trip uke into the throw. If you miss the early point, you can always continue the prop and increase the power of your upper body pull to drag uke over the balance point into the throw.

Inner thigh throw – Uchi mata

Description: From a lowered stance, tori turns leftwards away from uke and drives back with their right leg. The back of tori's right leg near the knee should drive upwards through uke's left inner thigh, lifting strongly. At the same time, tori pulls strongly forward and down in opposition to the upward drive of the leg. This lifts uke's left leg high enough pull both feet off the ground so that tori can complete the throw by pulling uke over tori's lifted left leg.

Common problems: Tori must ensure that uke's weight is committed to the front leg. Full commitment to the attacking sweep is vital.

Defensive value: Can be very effective with a left-arm underhook. An excellent way to attack uke's lead leg if tori has set their stance correctly before uke enters. Works best against shorter attackers, however. Can be made stronger by driving the leg through the groin, rather than carefully attacking just the inner thigh.

Counters:
- Uke can strengthen their grip, yield to tori's *kuzushi*, and drop strongly into *yoko guruma*.
- Alternately, if tori doesn't set up the throw correctly uke can easily lower their weight and drive for *ushiro goshi*.

Combinations:
- If uke resists the leg lift, tori can shift balance and change the *kuzushi* to try for *o uchi gari*.
- If uke successfully disengages the leg, tori can shift across farther and try for *ashi guruma* or even *tai otoshi*.

Notes:
- This is a difficult throw for smaller or shorter people to carry off. It can be challenging to lift uke high enough with the inner thigh attack.
- Even when this throw is successful, it often brings both players to the mat in competition. In self-defense it should be reserved for attacking shorter opponents.
- In an attack situation, *uchi mata* can effectively be used against the lead leg if tori's stance favours the move. If uke has over-extended their lead leg, this throw can work by attacking the inner thigh with a strong, thrusting sweep much lower, near the angle of the knee.
- When *uchi mata* is carried off successfully, the fall is quick with rapid body rotation that can slam an opponent to the ground.

Hip throws – Koshi waza

As the name suggests, hip throws generally topple uke over tori's hip. To achieve that, tori must isolate and extend the hip by pushing it out. Tori must also keep uke quite close, generally by being in front, body to body, and controlling uke's upper body with the grip.

In order to topple uke over the hip, uke's centre of gravity has to be higher than tori's hip. This is achieved in two ways. First, tori takes a low stance by bending their knees. This is important. As a rule of thumb, tori should look to have their belt lower than uke's and they need to bend their knees (keeping their back straight and head upright) until that is the case.

The second means of getting uke's centre of gravity over tori's hip is by means of the grip, and it is here that most of the variety in the hip throws occurs. For the most part, the *kuzushi* for the hip throws is an upwards and forwards pull, toppling uke forward on their toes. In that position, uke's balance is weak and if tori can quickly get the hip into position, the throw becomes easy.

Finally, in judo almost all hip throws are taught from the inside. That is, from the standard grip, with tori between uke's arms. The two exceptions are *utsuri goshi* and *ushiro goshi*, which start with tori behind uke. However it is worth knowing that some of the hip throws can be done from the outside. To achieve this, tori must be outside uke's arm, and must extend the hip across under the arm while bringing uke up and over for the throw.

There are two advantages to this. First, being outside the arm means it's difficult for uke to grab hold or strike back. Secondly, if tori controls uke's arm across tori's body, it is possible to use a powerful *ude gatame* (arm bar) to force uke into co-operating with the throw.

This use of a joint lock to coerce the throw and potentially damage uke's arm is illegal and unethical in judo. It is, however, classic old-school ju jutsu and quite effective as a defensive technique.

Note that the need to get your centre of gravity – and your hips! – under your opponent means that hip throws are less suited to taller persons. A tall person with a shorter opponent will need to lower their centre of gravity by bending the knees, and by widening the stance. Modern judo emphasises a narrow, meta-stable stance for throwing, but this puts tremendous strain on the knees. For defense purposes, a wider stance works just as well. It is easier for beginners to learn to 'centre' themselves on their opponents with a narrow stance, however, as all you really need to do is ensure you have put your two feet close together in the centre of the opponent's feet.

Being centred on your opponent is important for the hip throws. Beginners often position themselves to one side or the other, making it simpler for an opponent to escape, and requiring much more force to achieve the throw. Care must be taken when using a wider stance to be certain you are properly centred.

Major hip throw – O goshi

Description: Tori steps in and across with the right foot, turning away from uke and sliding their right arm around uke's left hip to the back. Drawing uke's right sleeve strongly forward, upward and across tori's body, tori bends at the knees, keeping their back straight to lower their stance until their hips are well below uke's. To complete the throw tori pushes back with their hips and straightens their legs to pick uke up, while leaning forward and pulling uke around their body to roll them off their hip to the ground in front.

Common problems: Tori must be body-to-body with uke before lowering their stance and completing the throw. Tori must also be well centred, not standing to either one side or the other of uke's centreline. Tori must lower their weight by bending the knees, not leaning forward.

Defensive uses: Forms of o goshi can be quite effective against pushing attacks, or haymaker/hook type punches. It is a simple throw found in systems worldwide, and makes great use of uke's momentum and attacking energy.

Counters:
- Uke can sink into a lowered stance as tori enters, and counterattack with *ushiro goshi*
- Uke can step around tori's right leg with their own right leg in a circular move. If uke then pulls tori's upper body with a circular action around to uke's left, uke can attack with a very quick *ko soto gari*.

Combinations:
- If uke attempts to step around to the right, tori can respond by attacking into uke's hips with their right hip for *uki goshi*
- Tori can also use uke's attempt to step past by attacking with *harai goshi* or *ashi guruma*

Notes:
- Although not technically correct, *o goshi* can be strengthened if tori underhooks uke's left arm with their right.
- A vicious and effective form of *o goshi* can be done by tori sliding their left hip across instead of their right, and retaining uke's right arm across their chest for an *ude gatame* which can either dislocate the elbow, or simply coerce uke into the throw more effectively.
- If used as a defense, tori must align their stance to face their hips the same direction uke's hips are facing – not the way uke's upper body may be facing after throwing a punch.

Floating hip throw – *Uki goshi*

Description: As uke moves to tori's left, tori pivots, lowers their stance and drives with their right hip into uke's right hip. Tori's right arm goes around uke's back while their left arm pulls uke's right sleeve forward and across tori's body. Tori completes the throw by standing up to lift uke's feet off the ground while pulling uke's body over their hip, dropping them forward and to tori's right side.

Common problems: See *o goshi*. Note that tori's stance is not central to uke in this case, however. Uke's right foot is outside tori's stance while tori's left foot is slightly outside uke's stance on the opposite side.

Defensive value: This throw is useful in the same manner as *o goshi*. It's a good response to pushes, overhead attacks and horizontal swing attacks.

Counters: See *o goshi*.

Combinations:
- If uke pulls back, tori is in position to drive for *o uchi gari*.
- If uke lowers their stance, tori can slip their right foot around uke's left foot and behind, to set up for *sukui nage*.

Notes:
- In practical terms, *uki goshi* is what happens when you attempt a quick *o goshi* against a moving and resisting opponent. The quick, sharp drive of the hip into uke's hip area is effective in off-balancing, but not as clean or as effective in lifting uke.

Rear hip throw – *Ushiro goshi*

Description: Tori stands close behind uke (often as counter to an attempted throw by uke) and lowers their stance – knees bent, feet wide, back straight. Gripping uke's torso strongly, tori drives forward and up with their hips, straightening their legs and tossing uke upward. Tori completes the throw by withdrawing the left leg and using hand control to bring uke down sideways across tori's feet.

Common problems: If tori tries to lift uke using arm strength and back muscles, the throw will fail unless tori is much bigger than uke. The key to this throw is driving forward and upward with a powerful thrust of the hips.

Defensive value: *Ushiro goshi* is an excellent throw to use if tori has managed to get behind uke. It is also an excellent response to many grappling and throwing attempts. It is a simple, powerful and effective throw which does not require a grip on clothing.

Counters:
- If uke can turn to the right inside tori's grip, uke can try for *ko uchi gari*.
- If uke can shift their hips and slip one leg behind tori, uke can attempt *sukui nage*.

Combinations:
- If uke lowers their stance to prevent the throw, tori can move to the right and bring their right leg across in front of uke to set up for *tani otoshi*
- If uke shifts their hips and slides one leg behind tori, tori can turn and attempt *o uchi gari* or *ko uchi gari*

Notes:
- Done with the correct use of hips and core muscles, it is possible to throw a person much larger than yourself. But incorrect lifting technique can cause serious injury to the back muscles.

Hip wheel – *Koshi guruma*

Description: Tori moves in front of uke and passes their right arm up and around uke's neck, placing their hand on the back of uke's shoulder. Tori bends at the knees, and pulls uke over and around using their left hand grip on uke's sleeve and the right arm around uke's neck. Straightening their legs to help lift uke, tori bends at the waist and wheels uke across their back using the hand grips.

Common problems: In judo, and for safety in training, tori must not lock the arm around uke's neck. This is the purpose of placing the hand on uke's shoulder. Tori must be body-to-body with uke before bending at the waist and attempting the throw.

Defensive value: This is a powerful throw. The neck grip offers great control over uke, especially if it is used as a headlock grip rather than the more open hand-on-shoulder version. However, retaining a strong grip on uke's neck while twisting and throwing can cause very serious injury. Care must be taken using this throw in self defense.

Counters:
- Uke can reach down right-handed to grip tori's belt, take a strong hold at tori's collar with their other hand, and drop to their right shoulder in front of tori to attempt *yoko guruma*.
- Uke can slip under tori's right arm and position themselves for *ushiro goshi*.

Combinations:
- If uke tries to step around, tori can drive their right leg back to catch uke's left inner thigh and attempt *uchi mata*.
- If uke slips their head free, tori can retain the grip on the right arm, shoot their right leg back, and drop into *soto makikomi*

Notes:
- A strong throw, but the requirement for arm around neck makes it a challenge for a smaller tori with a large uke.
- The neck grip is very powerful, especially if it becomes a headlock – but it poses safety issues in training.

Sweeping hip – *Harai goshi*

Description: Tori turns to their left and slips their right hip in front of uke driving up and to the left with their right hand, and pulling uke's left arm across to the left and down. Centring themselves in front of uke, tori lowers their stance and sweeps powerfully back and across uke's legs with their right leg while continuing to pull uke down and around to the left. The leg sweep continues through as tori leans strongly forward, balancing on their left foot.

Common problems: Over-reliance on the sweeping action can lead to failure. Tori must insure they are body-to-body, back straight, using powerful *kuzushi* and must get their hips below uke's by a combination of drawing uke forward and up, and by sinking down into their own stance before executing the sweep.

Defensive value: A very strong and effective throw. Useful against overhead and round/hook attacks, pushes and pulls. The jacket isn't necessary: a grip on uke's left arm and a good right-arm underhook work better anyway. The leg sweep keeps uke from slipping around to escape, and by lifting uke's legs high, tori makes uke's fall extremely jarring.

Counters:
- Uke lowers their stance, slips tori's grip and attacks with *ushiro goshi*.
- Uke steps quickly around with their right leg and attacks with *tani otoshi*.

Combinations:
- As uke tries to step around, tori changes line and drives their right leg sweep back into uke's left inner thigh for *uchi mata*
- Tori widens their stance by extending the right leg and sweeps for *ashi guruma*.

Notes:
- *Harai goshi* favours taller people with long legs. It can be difficult to carry off against a significantly taller opponent.

Sleeve lift and pull hip – *Sode tsurikomi goshi*

Description: From the standard grip, tori pulls uke's right arm up by the sleeve at the elbow and steps forward on the left foot. Pulling uke's right sleeve across and upwards, tori completes the turn to the right and settles in front of uke facing the same way, in close contact. Tori bends at the knees to lower their stance and uses the handgrip to pull uke over their left hip, while straightening their legs to lift uke off the ground for the throw. Tori completes the throw by using the handgrip to pull uke all the way around and over their left hip.

Common problems: Tori must have their left hand under uke's right elbow and push upward to start the throw. As the throw continues, tori must push strongly up and forward with the left hand, keeping it in front of their face and shoulder the whole way. If the left hand does not stay forward, tori's *kuzushi* will lack power and fail.

Defensive value: By definition this throw relies on uke wearing a strong jacket. It is possible to do the throw with grips to arms alone, but unless tori is much stronger than uke, it's easy for uke to slip out of such a grip. If a jacket is available, though, it offers a great deal of leverage and the throw becomes quite strong.

Counters:
- Uke can shoot their right leg behind tori, and yield to the pull on the sleeve. By bending in the middle, uke will quickly be in position to attack with *sukui nage*.
- Uke can slip the grip on their right sleeve and take a grip of their own on tori's right sleeve. Taking advantage of tori's pull across the body, uke can shift across and turn to their left, pushing tori's left sleeve high and pulling it across to attack with *sode tsurikomi goshi* on the opposite side.

Combinations:
- If uke slips the sleeve grip, tori can continue the turning motion and attack with left-side *koshi guruma* instead.
- If uke pulls up to escape the sleeve grip, tori can quickly turn back and attack strongly with *ippon seoi nage*.

Notes:
- The opposite-side version of this throw works nicely too, but you have to slip uke's grip on your right sleeve and acquire a grip on their left sleeve to start the throw off.

Lifting and pulling hip throw – *Tsurikomi goshi*

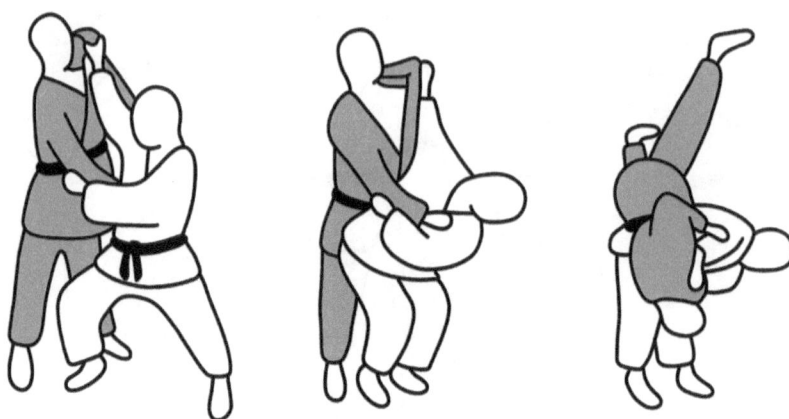

Description: Tori turns left and moves in towards uke while punching strongly upward with their right hand collar grip. Staying as close as possible to uke, tori continues the turn and bends at the knees to lower their stance until they face the same way as uke. Tori continues to forcefully extend their right hand with the collar grip, driving uke up, around and over as tori pushes back with their hips and straightens their legs to complete the throw.

Common problems: With the right arm extended, tori has to bend their knees deeply to make this throw work. The extended arm must remain forward, in front of tori's shoulder or tori will lose leverage and be unable to pull uke through the throw.

Defensive value: *Tsurikomi goshi* relies on uke wearing a strong jacket. Further, it demands that tori drop into a squat. Finally, if uke is shorter than tori the squat position necessarily becomes so deep that tori is almost sitting on their own heels. This is not a great throw for self defense.

Counters:
- Uke can attack with a left-foot *ko soto gari* as tori enters. Tori's raised arm allows for leverage making tori more vulnerable.
- Uke can lock onto tori's right hand with their right hand, turn towards their right and lower their balance to attack with *waki gatame*

Combinations:
- If unable to raise the right hand grip high enough, tori can push their right elbow under uke's right armpit and attempt *morote seoi nage*.
- If the right hand grip is weakened or lost, tori can release it altogether and wrap around uke's right arm for *soto makikomi*

Notes:
- A poor throw for taller practitioners.
- Requires considerable technical expertise to carry off well

Spring hip – *Hane goshi*

Description: In the standard grip, tori pulls uke up and forward. Turning quickly to the left, tori bends their right leg at the knee and drives in, attacking with their right hip. As tori enters, they lower their stance by sinking down on the left leg a little. When tori's hip strikes uke's front right hip area, tori also kicks back and through with the bent right leg, catching the inside of uke's right leg and pushing it back and outward. With uke's balance broken, tori continues to pull while leaning forward and driving high with the bent right leg to complete the throw.

Common problems: As tori has only one leg to stand on in this throw, it's vital that the left foot be placed centrally to provide support for the throw. If the foot is out of position, the throw will fail.

Defensive value: This is an attacking throw which can be carried out with an underhook. The issue of balancing on one foot is a problem, but if tori chooses they can strongly attack uke's right knee with the unbalancing sweep, potentially doing serious damage.

Counters:
- As tori turns to their right, uke can shift posture and attack with *o soto gari*
- Once tori is almost in position, uke can lower their stance and attack with *ushiro goshi*

Combinations:
- If uke resists by withdrawing their right leg, tori can pivot farther to the right and attack with *o uchi gari*
- If uke pulls away on their right leg, tori can change the sweep to the left inner thigh for *uchi mata*

Notes:
- The bent-leg lifting sweep of the right leg needs precision and timing. This is a difficult throw to carry off.
- It does lend itself as a combination when uke tries to step to the right around any of the other hip throws.

Changing hip throw – *Utsuri goshi*

Description: Uke enters and attempts a hip throw, so that tori is behind uke and pressed close. Tori lowers their stance, changes grip to control uke's torso, and bumps forward and upward with their hips to swing uke's feet clear of the ground. With uke's weight and balance now controlled by tori's grip, tori both swings uke into position and shifts their own stance to place uke on their own hip, ready to complete the throw as a standard hip throw.

Common problems: Requires good timing. Also it is essential for tori to use their legs and hips to drive uke forward and up. Trying to deadlift uke using the arms and the back muscles is not only unlikely to succeed, but may lead to serious injury.

Defensive value: Technically a good counter to common hip-throw attacks, but the need for good timing and the complexity of the finishing move makes it more showy than useful. *Ushiro goshi* is usually a simpler and more effective response in most circumstances.

Counters:
- Uke can lean into the throw, change their grip and attempt *yoko guruma*.
- Uke can dodge around the hip bump, change stance and attempt *sukui nage*.

Combinations:
- If uke tries to slip around the hip bump, tori can attack with *o uchi gari* as uke seeks a better stance.
- If uke lowers their stance to resist the hip bump, tori can step around to the left and attack with a right foot *ko uchi gari*.

Notes:
- A showy and complex throw. It can be attempted from a surprising number of positions in a judo competition, however.
- The basic hip-bump to unbalance is a powerful technique that applies well to self defense.

Sacrifice throws – Sutemi waza

Sacrifice throws are so called because tori goes to ground with uke. Tori actively sacrifices their own balance and position to bring uke to the ground in an inferior position.

Sacrifice throws depend on commitment. Tori must strongly and actively commit their weight and balance to the throw. Half-measures not only lead to failure, but can cause injury by bringing uke down on top of tori in an incomplete throw.

There is a lot of value in sacrifice throws. By bringing all of tori's weight to bear on the throw, it is possible for a small person to throw someone much larger using sacrifice techniques. Furthermore, many sacrifice throws work when you're already offbalanced by your opponent: being pushed, pulled, or even tripped and thrown. If your own balance is already compromised, it makes a lot of sense to attempt a sacrifice throw that will bring your opponent down to the ground with you, but on your own terms.

Despite this, in actual conflict going to the ground with your opponent is usually not desirable unless you are absolutely certain that nobody is going to step in to help your opponent. Once you're on the ground it takes time and space to regain your feet. If someone else is at hand, ready to kick you in the head or hit you with whatever comes to hand, going to the ground is a poor choice.

Sacrifice throws can also be a useful way to throw a larger or more powerful person. The full commitment of weight and energy involved gives tori considerable leverage. Be careful, though. Attempting a sacrifice throw against a person of much greater size and strength than you can leave you dangling foolishly in mid-air if your opponent is properly braced.

Crab claw (scissors) throw – *Kani basami*

Description: Can be done from either side. Tori releases the grip with one hand, and turns away from uke to stand side-by-side. Tori places the palm of the free hand on the ground for support, and kicks out at uke with both legs. Tori's higher leg goes across uke's hips in front. Tori's lower leg goes across uke's calves and ankles from behind. Tori then twists their body strongly in the direction of the upper leg, forcing uke to fall backwards over the lower leg.

Common problems: If tori doesn't commit to the jump to get their legs into position, uke will have time to move. Tori must move as close as possible in the jump so the strongest part of their legs is engaged in the throw. ALSO NOTE: position of the lower leg is critical. If it is behind the knee, there is a strong chance of injuring uke badly. THIS THROW IS BANNED IN JUDO COMPETITION DUE TO INJURIES.

Defensive value: It's always questionable to take the fight to the ground unless you're sure that your opponent has no assistance nearby. However, *kani basami* is a quick, effective and aggressive means of overthrowing uke. For an untrained person the fall is dangerous. The body and head go straight back, and uke can easily slam the back of their head into the ground, or any nearby obstacles. Dangerous, effective throw.

Counters:
- As tori releases their grip, uke can attack with *ko soto gari* or *de ashi harai* before tori drops to attacking position.
- As tori releases their grip, uke can quickly shift behind them for *ushiro goshi* or *sukui nage*

Combinations:
- Tori can release their grip and move out, then turn sharply back inward to unbalance uke for *seoi nage*
- Tori can release the grip, then slide back in to attack with *ashi guruma*

Notes:
- It is possible to do this throw by jumping into position with the legs first, using your hand grip on uke to hold yourself until you can catch yourself with the other hand as you drop.
- Great care must be taken in training. There is a long history of injury to uke from this throw. Ensure your leg position is absolutely correct before completing the throw.

Outer winding throw – *Soto makikomi*

Description: From the standard grip, tori turns sharply left, throwing their right arm over uke's right arm and putting their right foot outside uke's right foot. Tori continues to turn, pulling uke's right arm down and across tori's body and wrapping tori's right arm over the top of uke's right arm. Tori leans strongly forward, dropping their weight on uke's trapped arm, and completes the throw by pulling uke forward and rolling them to the right.

Common problems: Tori must get the right foot outside uke's stance, and must fully commit their weight to the wrapped-up arm as they fall into the throw.

Defensive value: *Soto makikomi* is a powerful throw. As both arms are used to trap and wrap uke's one right arm, the jacket grip isn't necessary. By committing their weight to the throw, tori has the ability to overbalance and throw much larger people. Tori can also choose to simply drop to one knee and not follow uke to the ground – or tori can roll with uke, landing on uke's ribs as both hit the ground. Excellent throw for dealing with a classic haymaker attack.

Counters:
- Uke can step around, yield to the pull, and drop into a *sumi gaeshi*
- If tori doesn't commit weight to the throw, uke can pull back and attack with standing *kata ha jime*

Combinations:
- If uke steps around tori's right leg, tori can shift balance and attempt *o uchi gari* or *ko uchi gari*
- If uke resists the pull, tori can reverse direction and attempt *kuchiki taoshi*

Notes:
- A nasty version of this throw is *hane* makikomi, or spring winding throw. With this throw, the leg entry is the same as for *hane goshi*, while the arm and upper body action are as *soto makikomi*. The major difference to the outcome is that tori no longer has support from their right leg to guide the fall. They spin in the air with uke, and drop with their bodyweight onto uke's ribs. It's a brutal throw, a bludgeoning fall, and it's hard to avoid breaking uke's ribs.

Circular throw – *Tomoe nage*

Description: Can be done from standard grip, but it's easier if tori shifts the left hand up uke's sleeve closer to the collar. Tori takes a strong grip, and shoots their left leg between uke's legs, falling back and pulling uke. As tori falls, their right foot comes up to settle just below uke's belt to the left of uke's centreline. Tori continues the fall with a rolling motion, pulls uke's upper body over and down, and pushes up strongly with the right leg to throw uke up and over tori's head. Tori retains the grip to ensure uke lands on their back.

Common problems: Tori must commit to the drop. Tori must try to place their hips close to uke's feet, in the centreline. Tori's right foot must not be placed too high, above uke's centre of gravity.

Defensive value: *Tomoe nage* is a strong throw. It does depend on a solid upper-body grip which needs a jacket – but in an emergency, tori could grab uke's hair or even an ear to bring them into the fall. And while the throw is practiced with tori's right foot off the centreline of uke's body during the throw, it's actually easier to plant the foot in the groin and push strongly – even kick through – from that spot. An excellent throw to use if you are being pushed.

Counters:
- If uke is quick enough to realise what's going on, it's easy to step through for *o soto gari* or step around for *ko soto gari*.

Combinations:
- If uke pulls back before tori can fall, tori can attack with *o uchi gari* or *ko uchi gari*

Notes:
- Sacrifice throws require full commitment for efficacy and safety. *Tomoe nage* is scary for learners, and for their uke too. The best practice is to commit fully to the throw and go through with it.
- If tori is smaller than uke, the throw can be attempted by taking a strong grip, planting the right foot in uke's midsection, and pushing up and out to swing down, shooting the left leg between uke's legs as the fall happens. This method is risky but highly effective against a standing uke, rather than one who is pushing forward.

Corner throw – *Sumi gaeshi*

Description: From the standard grip, tori falls back and down allowing the left leg to pass between uke's feet. Tori's right foot hooks behind uke's knee, pushing uke's thigh up and over as tori continues the fall to the ground and draws uke over. Tori should release their right hand but retain the left-hand grip and kick up strongly against uke's left thigh with their right foot as uke goes over. This asymmetric pressure (pulling uke's right sleeve, while kicking uke's left leg up and away) will turn uke as they fall so they land at tori's upper left corner – hence the name 'corner throw'.

Common problems: Tori must fall close below uke's centre of gravity. The kick up and out with the right foot is critical and it must lodge behind the knee, not at the groin.

Defense value: This throw is an excellent response to attempted tackles and leg-grab takedowns. It's easier to carry off than *tomoe nage* because the right foot position is easier to achieve, and it throws uke to one side rather than straight over, making it easier to follow up with ground attacks.

Counters:
- If uke can step around to either side, tori will just fall down. No throw required. But if tori is quick enough to regain balance, uke can attack with *ko soto gari*, *o soto gari*, *o soto guruma* and *de ashi harai*.

Combinations:
- If uke is quick enough to step around on either side, tori can adjust to attack with *ko uchi gari* or *o uchi gari*.

Notes:
- Can be done from close up if an attacker is trying for a leg takedown or tackle. Tori should reach over with the right hand to anchor on uke's belt, or anything else handy.
- Works quite well with tori's left leg outside uke's right during the fall. In fact, tori's left thigh can act as a 'prop' preventing uke taking a stabilising step forward, making it easier to throw them over and to tori's left.

Valley drop – *Tani otoshi*

Description: From the standard grip, tori steps around uke, extending their left leg behind uke's legs. Retaining a grip on uke's upper body, tori executes a left-side break-fall, dropping as close as possible to uke's feet and pulling uke backward across tori's left leg.

Common problems: Tori must ensure to extend their leg behind uke, not at the side. The leg should fall parallel to an imaginary line which would connect uke's two feet. Tori must try to drop as close as possible to uke to get the best results.

Defensive value: This is an effective takedown, especially if tori lowers their stance and changes the grip to a bear-hug. It does take tori to the ground, however, so it should be used only where absolutely necessary.

Counters:
- Uke can lower their stance and take tori's right leg for *o uchi gari* or even *uchi mata*

Combinations:
- Tori can drop into *tani otoshi* from an attempt at *ko soto gari*

Notes:
- This is a good response to a puncher if you don't feel you can handle them while standing. Cover your head, slip in under a right-hand strike, grab the body and shift to the side and behind for *tani otoshi*.

Rear throw – Ura nage

Description: Tori lowers their stance and slips behind uke, gripping the torso from behind. Driving strongly upward with the hips, tori pulls uke up and back, ensuring that uke's centre of gravity is lifted higher than their own. Tori collapses in a left side break-fall while continuing to throw uke over their shoulder with the torso trip to finish the throw.

Common problems: This throw is often done from the front, virtually as a wrestler's suplex. It's quite dangerous off the mat. If tori arches their back too much, they can land on their head instead of their shoulders. If tori doesn't control uke's fall, uke may land on tori's head or neck. The drive of the hip is crucial, and turning to the side in the break fall instead of dropping back flat onto the shoulders makes it safer and easier to throw uke over the left shoulder.

Defensive value: In the classic judo *Nage No Kata*, this throw is done as a response to an overhead strike. Tori accepts uke's charge and falls back to their shoulders, throwing uke directly behind themselves. While this is reasonably safe with two skilled practitioners on the mat, doing it on a hard surface against a resistant opponent in the unpredictable arena of a fight is a poor idea. There are better, safer throws.

Counters:
- Uke can lower their stance if tori gets behind and attack with *kubi nage* or *ashi guruma*

Combinations:
- If uke resists a hip throw by stepping around, tori can attack with *ura nage* from behind. Although to be honest, *ushiro goshi* is safer and just as effective.

Notes:
- It is valuable to understand that by using your opponent's momentum, you can throw them in almost any direction. Some directions are much less useful than others, however. Throwing someone backwards over your head (as in the classic kata version of this throw) is risky on many levels.
- Probably best to save practicing this throw until both uke and tori have a couple years experience on the mat, at the very least.
- The basic concept of getting your hips under and driving up and back is pretty simple. Versions of this throw appear in many street fight videos of complete amateurs. It's worth practicing defenses and counters.

Side drop – Yoko gake

Description: From the standard grip, as uke moves forward on the right foot, tori draws uke strongly up and forward to get uke onto their toes. At the same time, tori drives with the sole of the left foot at uke's right ankle, trying to push it across uke's body. Tori retains the left-hand grip on uke, and commits to the left-foot attack on uke's ankle by falling in a left-side break fall, allowing tori's bodyweight to add to the left-hand pull on uke's upper body.

Common problems: If uke isn't properly lifted up and forward, the attack on the ankle may simply turn into a kick that achieves nothing.

Defensive value: If the attack to the ankle is powerful, it can sweep uke's feet making the fall quite hard. It's a reasonable way to take a large, strike-oriented opponent to the ground with you if you really feel the need to go to the ground.... but on the other hand, a good *ko soto gari* or even *de ashi harai* will drop your opponent and leave you on your feet, ready to fight. Like many sacrifice throws, *yoko gake* is useful mostly in competition.

Counters:
- Uke can keep the front foot light and lift it around or over the sweeping attack. That leaves tori open to *ko soto gari*, *de ashi barai*, and even *yoko gake*.

Combinations:
- If uke plants heavily on the front foot, tori can swing farther around while dropping to attempt *tani otoshi*.

Notes:
- Handy in competitions. Distinctly limited use in defense.

Side wheel – *Yoko guruma*

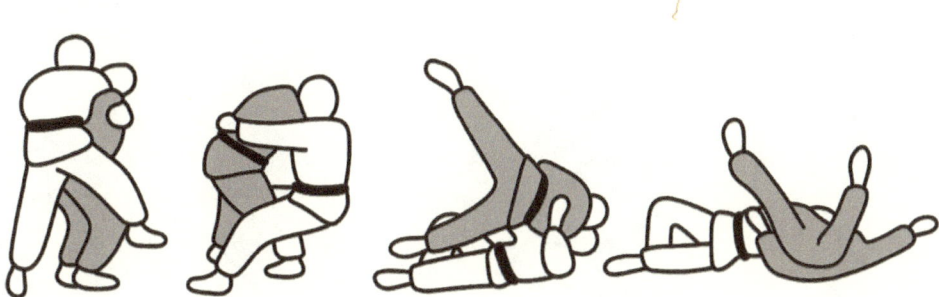

Description: Most often done as an escape from something like a shoulder or hip throw, *yoko guruma* usually starts with tori behind uke. Tori steps around with one foot, turning almost to face uke. Tori's leading hand is placed low on uke's front. A belt grip is good. Tori's rear hand is placed higher on uke's back. A collar grab is effective. Tori executes a side break fall onto their trailing leg, dropping their hips to the floor as close as possible to uke's feet. Tori's lead hand pushes up into uke's body while the hand on the back pulls uke over and around. Tori's fall allows their body weight to accelerate uke into the fall.

Common problems: *Yoko guruma* requires complete commitment. To use their body weight correctly, tori must enter and complete the turn-and-drop body movement fluidly and without pause. Dropping as close as possible to uke's feet is critical, as it makes the throw safe for tori, allowing uke to fall easily over tori's body instead of on top of it.

Defensive value: From uke's viewpoint, *yoko guruma* is a fast and highly disorienting throw, which is useful to tori. And while going to the ground isn't ideal in a defensive scenario, *yoko guruma* (and variations) is a very handy response if you find yourself being pulled forward, off balance. By yielding to the attacker's energy you can put it to your own ends, making the throw even more powerful.

Counters:
- Uke can drive back, attacking tori's trailing leg with *uchi mata* as tori attempts to step around.
- Uke can also turn with tori, and attempt *ashi guruma*.

Combinations:
- If tori is attempting *ushiro goshi* and uke resists by pulling forward, there is an opportunity to attack with *yoko guruma*.
- Can also be used if uke defends by stepping forward out of *sukui nage*.

Notes:
- Because of the starting position (tori behind uke) this is a good counter to a wide range of throws in sporting situations.

Side separation – Yoko wakare

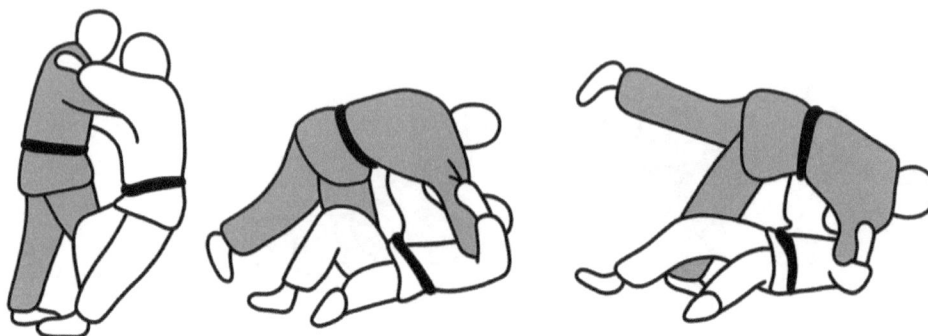

Description: Tori pushes uke up and back, provoking uke to resist with forward motion. As uke pushes forward, tori drops into a side break fall, landing their hips as close as possible to uke's leading foot. Pulling sharply down on uke's sleeve, tori pushes up and over with the opposite hand as they fall, tossing uke into a roll over tori's upper body.

Common problems: As with all the sacrifice throws, tori must be completely committed to the fall and must fall as close as possible to uke's feet. Falling outward, away from tori's feet will lead to uke landing on tori in the fall. Only by dropping close to uke's feet can tori ensure that uke will fall clear.

Defensive value: Again, going to the ground is usually not ideal. However, if you are off-balanced in a grappling situation, *yoko wakare* is a quick, efficient way of ensuring your attacker also hits the ground, and that you control the situation.

Counters:
- Uke can quickly lower their stance and attempt *sukui nage* before tori starts the fall.
- Uke can also attempt a quick *ko soto gari* as tori moves into position for the throw.

Combinations:
- If uke resists by pulling back, tori can switch stance and attempt *o soto gari*.
- If uke pulls away from tori's grip, tori can turn and grip uke's lead arm, attempting either *seoi nage* or *soto makikomi*.

Notes:
- Similar in many ways to *yoko guruma*. Distinct in that it's done from the front and both legs extend across uke's path, while in *yoko guruma* there's a more obvious 'spiraling' action to the fall and only one of tori's legs usually extends across uke's path.

Rice bag reversal – *Tawara gaeshi*

Description: Uke lowers their head and drives forward for *morote gari* or *kuchiki taoshi*. Tori widens their stance and bends to wrap uke's torso with both arms. Tori uses uke's forward impetus, gets their feet under uke's centre of gravity, and with bent knees (wide, low stance) topples back, hauling uke up and over. Tori turns their body and angles uke's fall to throw uke to a back corner.

Common problems: Tori must not attempt to straighten and lift uke for the throw as this will put dangerous strain on tori's back. Tori must relax, sit back and down while maintaining close contact with uke's torso by means of the wraparound arm grip. It is crucial that tori turns their body and angles uke's fall to prevent uke falling directly on tori's face.

Defensive value: If you are completely confident about being able to fall backwards safely in the environment of a fight, *tawara gaeshi* is an excellent response to common tackling-type attacks. It can be further improved if tori retains the torso grip and rolls back over their own shoulder as uke falls, because this allows tori to roll directly into a superior mount position that straddles uke's body. From here, tori can easily dominate the conflict.

Counters:
- *Tawara gaeshi* is itself a counter, relying on uke taking a vulnerable position. Once tori's arms are locked, it's quite difficult to counter this with another throw. Any counter to *tawara gaeshi* needs to happen early – preferably by attacking correctly and powerfully from the outset so as to avoid being thrown in *tawara gaeshi* altogether.

Combinations:
- Again, *tawara gaeshi* happens when uke takes a very particular line of attack. Combining this with another throw isn't simple. If uke resists by pulling back from the torso grip, tori can 'sprawl' forward, drop their weight onto uke's torso, and simply drive uke to the ground. If uke attempts to stand up, tori can shift the grip with one hand and attempt a form of *kuchiki taoshi*.

Notes:
- *Tawara gaeshi* is strongly disorienting for most attackers. Their plan of attack involves tackling tori. Being suddenly and violently hurled into what is almost a front flip usually comes as a surprise, and gives tori a few vital instants in which to finish the conflict.

Hand throws – Te waza

These throws are grouped together because the finishing elements are driven by action of the hands and arms. As practiced in judo (and many schools of ju jutsu) there is a strong element of dependency on the uniform jacket, which means that some of these throws appear to have limited value in self defense.

It is worth remembering that Kano Jigoro put considerable time and effort into recreating dangerous throws for his 'judo' system so they could be trained safely, and taught easily to beginners. Many of the hand throws can be done from joint-locking techniques once you understand the basics of balance and entry, and as such they can be performed with devastating results.

Throwing a partner with a joint-lock in place is no simple matter, however. Both partners need to be skilled and comfortable with *ukemi*, and tori must have real control over the throw, including the ability to relax the joint-lock at any point through the technique.

Not all systems of ju jutsu include joint-locking variations of the common throws. I have included pointers on a few of them here, but I can't stress enough that joint-locked throwing techniques present a real risk of injury. They should be practised only with the greatest of care.

In judo, the practice of *randori* (competitive grappling and throwing) allows for the development of tactical skill and a deep understanding of how weight and momentum integrate with throwing techniques. However for defense, this isn't enough. If you only understand throws from a grappling perspective, it will be difficult to use them when your opponent is striking and kicking. The essence of ju jutsu is adaptability. If your opponent is striking and kicking skilfully, it is useful to change the situation and attack with grappling and throwing so as to take your opponent into an arena where they may be less skilled.

To do this, you must practice throws in the dojo from aggressive, attacking situations as well as from regular grappling situations. You need to be able to combine striking and kicking with your throwing. Classically, ju jutsu used strikes not as finishing techniques but as a means of distracting or off-balancing an opponent long enough to permit a powerful throw or destructive joint-lock attack. In modern times where attackers rarely wear armour, strikes are more effective than they were on a medieval Japanese battlefield. Nevertheless, it is often difficult to defend effectively with strikes alone. Throws are powerful weapons that damage your opponents on all levels: physically, psychologically and positionally. Learning to integrate throws with other defensive techniques is at the very core of the practice of ju jutsu.

One arm shoulder throw – *Ippon seoi nage*

Description: From the standard grip, tori pulls uke up and forward. Tori keeps their left-hand grip on uke's sleeve, but turns across uke's body and brings their right arm up and under uke's right arm, trapping it tightly in the bend of their elbow. Tori continues to turn and lower their stance by bending their knees until they stand directly in front of uke, pressed close. Keeping uke's trapped arm tightly held, tori leans their body forward and straightens their legs to lift their hips as uke falls forward. Tori completes the throw by pulling uke's right arm forward and around, lowering their own right shoulder to pull uke over and around.

Common problems: Tori must lock their right arm around uke's right arm close to uke's shoulder. Tori must not try to lift and pull uke into the throw with the arm. Instead, tori must ensure they are in front of uke, with a lower stance and a straight back, and pressed closely to uke. If tori does not keep a straight back and press close to uke, tori will have to drag uke up and over by sheer physical strength – which may not be sufficient if uke is strong and heavy.

Defensive value: *Ippon seoi nage* is a useful response to a strongly committed overhand or round-arm swing attack. However it is important to move quickly and commit fully to the throw. You want to use the attacker's momentum and energy to help the throw along. If you are slow or uncommitted, you put yourself in a dangerous position with your attacker close behind you where they can try to strangle, grapple, or strike at undefended targets.

Counters:
- *Yoko guruma* is an excellent counter to *ippon seoi nage*, and likewise *yoko wakare*.
- You can also try to slide around on the side of the trapped arm, and try to atack with *ko soto gari*.

Combinations:
- If uke escapes backwards by withdrawing their arm, tori can respond with *kuchiki taoshi*, or with *o uchi gari*.
- If uke attempts to step around the throw, tori can shift their grip on the right arm and drop into *soto maki komi*.

Notes:
- This classic throw is a staple of movies and television shows.

Two arm shoulder throw – *Morote seoi nage*

Description: Although usually taught distinctly and separately to *ippon seoi nage*, this throw is essentially the same, but tori retains the gi grip instead of releasing the right hand and underhooking uke's right arm. Tori drives uke upward and forward with the grip, then turns to the left sharply. Tori's right elbow slides under uke's armpit, and tori retains the right-hand collar grip. Tori's right elbow now provides powerful extra leverage as tori completes the turn, lowering their balance and then leaning forward to draw uke over their shoulder into the throw.

Common problems: Tori must ensure to lower their stance and get their centre of gravity under uke. Tori must keep body contact during the entry and unbalancing phase. It is vital that tori's right elbow move across freely to slide under uke's right armpit.

Defensive value: Relies on the jacket grip, making it more difficult to use the momentum of an incoming attack and of course, more difficult still with a jacket-less attacker.

Counters:
- See *ippon seoi nage*.

Combinations:
- See *ippon seoi nage*.

Notes:
- If tori begins from a position of gripping both of uke's wrists, tori can turn to the right and cross uke's arms over tori's right shoulder. Tori should ensure to turn uke's left hand palm upwards which allows for an *ude gatame* (straight arm lock) on uke's left arm, with the fulcrum at tori's right shoulder. Tori can now complete *morote seoi nage* as normal, with the added leverage of the painfully locked arm to help encourage uke to co-operate with the throw. Care must be taken during practice to avoid damage to uke's pinned and hyper-extended left elbow.

Shoulder wheel – *Kata guruma*

Description: From the standard grip, tori pulls strongly with their left hand on uke's sleeve, extending uke up and forward. At the same time, tori turns to the left and enters with bended right leg, right foot between uke's feet. Tori crouches and pulls uke with the extended arm onto their shoulders, standing up briefly as uke topples across their shoulders. Tori finishes the throw by circling the left hand, arm still extended, down and across their own knees while using the right hand to help throw uke's legs off to the left.

Common problems: Tori must enter as deeply as possible to get under uke's centre of gravity. It is vital that tori's back is straight, and vertical: if tori bends, uke's weight places immense strain on tori's spine. If tori does not keep full extension of their right arm and make a big circle across the front of their own body, they run the risk of dropping uke onto themselves, or at the very least making the fall very difficult for a training partner.

Defensive value: The standing version of this throw isn't easy to manage from this direction, but if tori drops their left knee to the ground as they move in, the throw becomes faster and easier. By dropping low under the arm, tori can try to use the power and momentum of a straight-line, overhead, or even round-arm right-hand punch from uke. The throw is disconcerting, and the fall is jarring even for trained persons.

Counters:
- Uke can slip tori's right-hand grab and attempt *de ashi harai* as tori enters.
- Uke can retain their own grip on tori and drop straight into *tani otoshi*.

Combinations:
- If uke turns their body and withdraws a leg to escape, tori can attack with either *o uchi gari* or *ko uchi gari*, whichever is appropriate.
- Uke can also enter more deeply and attack tori's lead leg with *uchi mata*.

Notes:
- The standard method of doing this throw, shown here, has tori entering from the inside line. In combat, though, if tori can take the outside line (by slipping a right hand grab, for example) tori can seize uke's right wrist, push it across uke's body as they enter from the outside line, and execute *kata guruma* this way. If this is done, the right arm will be locked in *ude gatame* across tori's back and shoulder. It is possible to damage the arm very badly in this way, which makes this version of *kata guruma* useful in defence.

Neck throw – *Kubi nage*

Description: From the standard grip, tori enters on the right leg. Tori's right arm goes up around uke's neck, like a headlock grip. Tori continues turning towards the left as the arm goes around the neck, unbalancing uke with the neck grip. Tori's right leg extends out and back, and as tori continues to pull uke around and downward with the neck grip, tori's right leg straightens and trips up uke to complete the fall.

Common problems: Tori cannot simply rely on the neck grip and strength – it is crucial to lower their stance and drive back with the right leg.

Defensive value: *Kubi nage* is a powerful defensive throw. The neck grab is a very 'natural' response for many people in a grappling situation. The right-arm entry can come from a block against a left-hand punch or attack, and as tori turns to take the grip, tori can smash down strongly with the right arm to lock in place around uke's neck. The throw across the leg allows tori to engage their body weight, and if tori chooses to retain the neck grip instead of releasing uke in the fall, tori can keep a strong neck-lock/headlock.

Counters:
- Uke can slip under the neck lock to get behind tori for *ushiro goshi* or *sukui nage*.
- Uke can also try to step around the right leg into *yoko guruma*.

Combinations:
- If uke slides under the neck grab early, tori can shoot their right leg behind and attempt *sukui nage*.
- If uke slips under the neck-lock but fails to disengage, tori can attempt *uchi mata* with the right leg.

Notes:
- There's considerable disagreement about this throw across different systems of judo and ju jutsu. This version uses a neck grip somewhat similar to *koshi guruma*, but the footwork and direction of throw is very similar to *tai otoshi*. Some schools would call this a *tai otoshi*. Others might call it a variation on *koshi guruma*. The naming problem is compounded by the fact that aikido includes a '*kubi nage*' which is radically different again...
- It is possible for tori to keep the neck grip and turn this throw into a sacrifice by dropping down onto uke. This allows near immediate entry to the *kesa gatame* hold-down.

Scooping throw – *Sukui nage*

Description: With their right leg, tori steps behind uke's lead left leg. Tori's right arm goes across uke's torso, seeking a grip around the waist. As tori steps deep with the right leg behind uke, tori lowers their stance and takes a grip behind uke's left thigh or knee. Driving forward and up with their hips, tori strongly lifts uke's leg, and drives uke back using the right arm and shoulder in a twisting motion to throw uke over backwards.

Common problems: Tori should lower the stance by bending their legs, not leaning forward. The more tori leans forward, the more potential strain on tori's spine in the lifting phase. The lift should come with an upward and forward push of tori's hips, not through the right arm.

Defensive value: *Sukui nage* is useful against common headlock attacks and attempts to pull tori around. It is also easy to use against bearhug-type attacks once the grip is broken.

Counters:
- As tori steps behind with the right leg, uke can attempt *ko soto gari* with their left leg. Uke can grab tori around the neck with their left arm and attempt a left-side *kubi nage* before tori lowers their stance far enough.

Combinations:
- If uke tries to escape by withdrawing the left foot, tori can prevent this with a right-leg *ko soto gari*.
- If uke manages to turn to face tori, tori can attack with either *kuchiki taoshi* or *morote gari*.

Notes:
- Judo is a sport, and points are scored for throwing your opponent such that both feet leave the ground. However it is possible to do a very effective version of this throw without lifting uke at all. Tori simply slides the right leg into position behind uke, extends their right arm across uke's torso at the level of the shoulders, and stands up while twisting to the right. The extended right arm drives uke's upper body back, while the right leg prevents uke stepping back, forcing uke to fall. This version of the throw is useful in self-defense.

Body drop – *Tai otoshi*

Description: From the standard grip, tori turns left and pushes uke up and to the left. Tori then pulls uke over and farther left while at the same time extending the right leg deeply across uke's legs. Tori finishes the throw by rotating their upper body and hips into a deep *zen kutsu dachi* (forward leaning stance) and straightening their right leg, throwing uke quickly over the extended leg.

Common problems: Tori needs to be in a deep, low stance to carry this throw off properly. It's important to get the right leg across early, and extend it properly.

Defensive value: *Tai otoshi* relies on a jacket grip, which diminishes its value for defense. However the fall is swift, abrupt and extremely jarring, making it very useful for disorienting an opponent. Nevertheless, for defense a deep *kubi nage* is likely to be more useful.

Counters:
- If uke can get a good left-hand grip on tori's back at belt or collar, *yoko guruma* or *yoko wakare* are useful counters.
- If uke lowers their stance quickly when tori first attempts the *kuzushi*, uke can slip behind tori to attempt *ushiro goshi*

Combinations:
- If uke tries to pull back or to step around, tori can drive back with the right leg for *uchi mata*
- If uke steps out around the right leg, tori can shift balance and attack with a right-leg *ko uchi gari*.

Notes:
- The fall is quick and jarring. In practice, uke is advised to jump into the fall and allow themself to spin quickly in the air to come down in a side break fall.

Floating drop – Uki otoshi

Description: Tori steps back deeply with the left leg, lowering their stance and pulling strongly on uke's right sleeve. As uke comes forward, tori swings the left leg back behind them, dropping into a kneeling posture, pulling uke around and over with the left hand while pushing at uke's left shoulder or collar with the right hand.

Common problems: Tori should not simply rely on the pull with the left arm. The two hands work together to perform this throw, like turning a wheel.

Defensive value: Another jacket-dependent throw, if done in this fashion. However it can work against a pushing opponent. It can also be done by tori striking hard with an open right hand at left side of uke's head or neck to offbalance. Tori then grabs onto the upper surface of the crook of uke's right elbow with tori's left hand. The throw can then be carried out in virtually identical fashion: tori pulls at uke's arm with the left hand, and pushes uke's head or neck with the right hand while tori turns and drops into the kneeling position. This is a powerful and effective defensive throw.

Counters:
- If uke can slip tori's left-hand grip, tori is open for *kuchiki taoshi* to the right leg.
- If uke steps quickly to their left before tori can pull strongly, uke can attack with *de ashi harai* or *ko soto gari*.

Combinations:
- If uke slips or pulls back, tori can enter strongly and take a right underhook grip for *ashi guruma* or *uchi mata*.

Notes:
- This is an excellent example of a fighting throw which has been rendered 'safe for training'. The defensive version with the strike to the side of uke's head and the left-hand grip on the elbow is quick, disorienting, powerful and effective no matter what uke may be wearing.

Two-handed reap – *Morote gari*

Description: Tori ducks in under uke's guard and uses their shoulder to attack uke's midriff. Tori reaches down and grips behind uke's knees, pulling uke's legs up on either side of tori's body while pushing forward with the shoulder to throw uke onto their back.

Common problems: Tori must not try to lift uke. The throw uses a reaping action. The pulling of the hands behind the knees works in opposition to the push from the shoulder, easily tipping uke. Trying to lift uke places strain on tori's spine.

Defensive value: *Morote gari* is a quick, simple throw easily put into action. However the version commonly taught (and depicted here) leaves tori vulnerable to instinctive neck grabs from even untrained attackers – and to dangerous and painful Guillotine Chokes from attackers with appropriate training.

Counters:
- The obvious counter to this throw is *tawara gaeshi*, the rice bag reversal.
- If uke is quick, it can also be countered by the simple expedient of pushing strongly down on tori's head and shoulders as tori enters. Uke can even throw their legs out behind and fall forward on tori, bringing tori to the ground under uke's weight – a technique called "sprawling".

Combinations:
- If uke attempts to escape by withdrawing one leg, tori can pursue and attempt *kuchiki taoshi*.
- If uke attempts to lean forward and 'sprawl', tori can try pushing in for a low *kata guruma*.

Notes:
- The sport/judo version of the throw depicted and described here has tori's head under uke's arm. Even untrained people will instinctively grip that arm around the neck when attacked in this way, and if they hold tightly the throw becomes dangerous for tori. Worse: a trained person can take the opportunity to apply a powerful and dangerous Guillotine Choke. To use this throw in defense, tori should attack with their head across uke's body, tucked into uke's midriff, rather than pushing under the arm.

Dead tree drop – *Kuchiki taoshi*

Description: Tori enters quickly on their right leg to the inside of uke's right leg and uses their left hand to scoop uke's right leg at the knee. Tori pushes uke away with their right hand, straightening up to lift uke's leg. Tori completes the throw by pushing uke back and across to their right while holding uke's right leg trapped. (As illustrated) ALTERNATIVE: Tori steps deep with their left leg to the outside of uke's right leg. Drawing uke's sleeve back, down and leftwards tori uses their right arm to scoop uke's right leg at the knee from the inside. Tori straightens and drives forward to lift uke's right leg, and continues the pull on uke's sleeve to complete the throw.

Common problems: Tori must unbalance uke with the opposite hand while making the entry for the scoop, or seize a moment when uke is already unbalanced. Simply bending and reaching for the leg invites a strong counterattack.

Defensive value: This is a versatile and easy throw. It isn't particularly dependent on uke's clothing, and it can be put into action against a wide variety of attacks, or used as an attack in its own right.

Counters:
- Uke can quickly slip the scooping grip and draw tori into *sumi gaeshi* by moving their right foot to the inside of tori's left knee.
- Uke can dislodge tori's right-shoulder push and plant their weight forward, using their left hand grip on tori's sleeve to draw them into *kata guruma*.

Combinations:
- If uke slips the scoop and withdraws their right leg, tori can attack with a right-leg *ko uchi gari*.
- If uke escapes the scoop at close range, tori can attack with *uchi mata*.

Notes:
- This throw is one of the 'modern' adoptions of the Kodokan Judo, but it is widespread across many martial systems.
- Powerful, simple and effective.
- Difficult for tori to help uke control the fall. In self-defense situations – especially against an untrained attacker – this throw can easily lead to uke striking their head sharply as they fall. This is dangerous from a legal standpoint.

Four direction throw – *Shiho nage*

Description: Tori stands at uke's right side, facing across uke's front. Tori grasps uke's right wrist in both hands. Right hand grabs close to the hand, thumb downwards. Left hand grasps farther up the forearm, thumb upwards. With extended arms, tori steps forward on the left foot to push uke's arm across the front of uke's body, then lift it. Lowering their head and holding uke's arm a little above, tori pivots 180 degrees by the right, twisting uke's arm overhead as they go. When the pivot move is complete, tori has uke's arm in a shoulder lock, with uke's wrist projecting forwards in front of tori at eye level. Tori completes the throw by sweeping down and to the right in a cutting motion with the gripped wrist, forcing uke to fall, or suffer a dislocation.

Common problems: Tori's grip must be strong and the arm action must be decisive to keep uke off-balance through the whole throw. The pivot action must be quick, and tori should keep uke's hand forward of tori's head throughout the 'turning under the arm' process.

Defensive value: Done correctly, this throw is devastating and destructive. It is easy to damage the shoulder joint so badly that uke can't use it.

Counters: Uke can turn quickly with tori at the 'under the arm' phase, preventing the lock. Uke can step forward and brace their arm against their body to prevent tori pushing it across in the first place. If uke can pivot with the arm push and finesse a grip on tori's right arm with their right hand, uke can attempt *kata guruma*.

Combinations: If uke shifts to resist the hand-attack, tori can attack with *ko soto gari* or *de ashi harai*.

Notes:
- This is a difficult and subtle throw that requires much practice. It's not much good against fast punches, but in the early phase of confrontation where the aggressor may attempt to grab or push, *shiho nage* can end things early and completely.
- This throw did not enter the judo curriculum created by Kano Jigoro. It is still found in aikido, as established by Ueshiba Morihei.
- Take great care in practice. *Shiho nage* produces powerful leverage on the arm, and it's all too easy to damage your practice partner.

Head turning throw – *Hachi mawashi*

Description: Tori achieves a head-control grip with the left hand at the back of uke's head, and the right hand cupping uke's chin. Tori pivots on the left foot away from uke, and uses the head grip to pull uke's head forward, down, and toward's tori's right. As uke attempts to resist the pulling, twisting action, tori reverses the pivot by stepping onto their right foot and turning to the left. Now, tori pushes sharply upwards and away on uke's chin, and pulls strongly on the back of uke's head with the left hand. With this quick reversal, tori unbalances uke and can simply twist and push uke's head back and down towards the left, taking uke to the ground.

Common problems: The pull-and-twist action on the uke's head must incorporate motion in several directions at once. The first part includes a forward-and-down component as well as a twist from uke's left to right. The second part includes and upwards-and-back component as well as a twist from uke's right to left. Merely twisting the head in one plane is likely to just annoy the hell out of uke. You need to overbalance them, so make sure you're working all the angles.

Defensive value: This is a nice, powerful throw that has the distinction of working at very close quarters. This is a something of a go-to response for me particularly when working against surprise attacks. By getting in close to the opponent you make it harder for them to score power strikes against you, and once you get strong head control they need to respond very quickly, or you can take them to the ground with little effort.

Counters: It's difficult to counter *hachi mawashi* with judo-style throwing if it's done with solid head control at close ranges. You may try to tuck your chin, and drive for a trip or a reap.

Combinations: If uke manages to tuck their chin to prevent the grip, you can continue driving in, pass your right arm over their left shoulder, get your hip tucked behind theirs, and attempt *irimi nage*.

Notes:
- Head control is really handy. Against most people, it's an extremely effective way to direct the fight any way you really want it to go.
- If you're worried about breaking somebody's neck with the head twist – yeah, no. You've seen too many movies. It can be done, sure, but you need to be strong, fast, fully committed, and most of all you need to know the trick. It's really not as easy to break a resisting adult's neck as the Jason Bourne movies would have you believe.

Entering throw – *Irimi nage*

Description: Uke advances on the right foot, reaching or striking with the right hand. Tori evades the strike by stepping to forward on their left foot, outside uke's right foot. As uke begins to recover their balance from the strike, tori shoots their right arm across uke's upper torso, elbow under uke's chin. Using uke's own "straightening up" movement, tori drives back and to the left with their right upper arm, folding the forearm down over uke's back. With tori's right hip now tucked neatly in against and behind uke's right hip, tori turns their body sharply to the left, bringing uke back and across into the fall.

Common problems: While the right arm does the job of guiding uke's head and upper body, the power for this throw comes from the footwork and body movement. If tori doesn't coordinate body movement with the arm, uke's balance will not be broken and the throw will fail. This throw requires good timing and a 'feel' for uke's balance and movement.

Defensive value: quite useful against a regular, untrained opponent. Difficult to pull off against the classic right haymaker punch, but can be done against straight strikes and grabs – so if uke tries to 'set up' the haymaker by reaching with the left, tori can use a left-hand *irimi nage* to take uke down.

Combinations: If uke manages to shift balance to resist the throw, there will be openings for any of several of the leg-tripping throws.

Counters: Uke can lock onto tori's arm and turn quickly and strongly for *morote seoi nage*

Notes:
- This is a bread-and-butter throw for aikido. They have many, many variations on it, some of which look spectacular – but require a lot of cooperation. Stick to the basic version. You'll be better off. This is a simple, powerful, easy throw which takes advantage of uke's commitment to their own attack, and turns their balance against them.

Back-bending throw

Description: Tori stands facing uke, on uke's right. Tori's right hand grabs uke under the jaw, forcing uke's head up and back. Tori's left hand braces against uke's back just above the hips, preventing uke from stepping backwards. Tori completes the throw by forcing uke's head back far enough that uke overbalances, and tori can deposit them on the ground.

Common problems: Hard to pull off on a much taller person. Requires real commitment to the head-pushing action.

Defensive value: Ultra-simple throw that can be done very quickly. If tori slaps their hand over uke's face instead of gently and kindly pushing up on the jaw, tori can use the nose to add painful leverage. The idea is to break uke's balance before they have time to realise what's going on and muster resistance to the throw. If done at the right moment of opportunity with plenty of commitment, this throw is very effective.

Counters: If uke ducks or slips to avoid the hand in the face, uke can attack with a range of throws. Slipping behind for *sukui nage* or *ushiro goshi* is effective.

Combinations: If uke successfully slips the hand grip by turning towards tori, tori can shift the left hand grip to catch uke's sleeve, arm or jacket and drop into *tani otoshi*, or *sumi gaeshi* if tori can get a grip with both hands.

Notes: This is a ridiculously simple throwing technique that requires just speed and commitment. I'm sure there's a good Japanese name for it somewhere, but I've never seen it. Use of face and head make the throw illegal in judo competition, and it does require an element of surprise so it doesn't show up in the ring, either – but as a means of taking a relatively untrained opponent to the ground with speed and control, this throw is worth knowing. It works on the simple principle that where the head goes, the body follows. Move the head fast enough (with pain to the nose, for example) and most people will overcommit their balance before they've even realised something is wrong.

Joint locking techniques – *Kansetsu waza*

Section one: Standing joint lock techniques	**75**
Armpit hold – *Waki gatame*	76
Arm entanglement – *Ude garami*	77
Reverse arm entanglement – *Ushiro ude garami*	78
Straight armlock – *Ude gatame*	79
Outwards forearm twist – *Kote gaeshi*	80
Wrist crush – *Te kubi hishigi*	81
Side wrist crush – *Yoko te kubi hishigi*	82
Forearm turnover – *Kote mawashi*	83
Forearm twist – *Kote hineri*	84
Reverse wrist crush – *Gyaku te kubi hishigi*	85
Section two: Joint locking techniques as ground restraints	**86**
Ground restraint – *Kote hineri*	87
Straight armlock ground restraint #1 – *Ude gatame*	88
Straight armlock ground restraint #2 – *Ude gatame*	89
Hanging wrist crush ground restraint – *Te kubi hishigi*	90
Double leg tie ground restraint	91
Spine lock ground restraint	92
Leg entanglement ground restraint – *Ashi garami*	93
Section 3: Joint lock techniques for ground-fighting	**94**
Scarf entanglement – *Kesa garami*	95
Grounded figure four arm entanglement – *Ude garami*	96
Cross armlock – *Juji gatame*	97
Armpit hold – *Waki gatame*	98
Grounded shoulder lock – *Gyaku ude garami/Ushiro ude garami/Kimura*	99
Leg-set reverse armlock – *Omoplata/ashi gatame*	100
Leg entanglement – *Ashi garami*	101

Joint locking techniques are common across many martial arts, including the HEMA (Historical European Martial Arts). Recent developments in professional MMA (mixed martial arts) and cage fighting have led some in the martial arts community to declare that most jointlocking techniques are impractical and ineffective, and simply wouldn't work in the context of genuine fighting. Despite these expert opinions, a remarkable number of technical manuals from the middle ages onward in Europe, written by professional fighters and killers who used weapons as well as empty hand techniques, clearly depict moves that any practitioner of ju jutsu today would recognize as wristlocks, armlocks and shoulder locks.

This is where the context of a martial art is important. I will not claim that joint-locking techniques are 'too dangerous' for the cage-fighting scene. But I will say that fighting in self defense is rarely, if ever, a neat match-up between two individuals of similar size, build and skill operating inside the strict limits of an otherwise empty fighting arena with excellent footing, good lighting, and a complete lack of weapons, obstacles, and bystanders. As ever, you should suit your choice of techniques to the conflict you are facing.

The simple fact is that joint-locking techniques are not generally meant to be used against a poised professional fighter throwing calculated, fast-moving strikes that don't commit their full body weight and momentum. Trying to catch a boxer's hand is completely stupid – unless the boxer foolishly decides to give you that hand in the first place.

But why would he do something like that? Let's put it another way: how many fights have you seen that start with someone pushing someone else's chest? Or poking someone with their index finger as a challenge? Both of those openings are extremely common – and both provide excellent opportunities to shut down the whole fight immediately by applying a joint-locking technique to the proffered hand or arm.

Most joint-locking techniques are relatively low percentage once both fighters have entered full combat mode. But in the leadup to combat there are frequently openings to use them. Further: most people begin their attack with what they expect to be a devastating strike. Statistically, this is usually a big, swinging right haymaker. Again: the big, committed strike represents an opportunity to respond with techniques that can shut the whole fight down immediately, such as joint locks and throws. Yet even if you find yourself caught in a stand-up fight, if you can distract, disrupt, offbalance or stun your opponent with a striking technique of some kind, you may find an opportunity to apply a joint lock technique.

The value of joint locking techniques is twofold. In less intense situations – for example, if you need to escort a drunk to the door and encourage him to leave – you can apply the jointlock early, and use pain to get compliance and cooperation. Security officers, doormen, police and others do this kind of thing routinely, and if the techniques are applied properly they're quite efficient.

However as matters heat up, joint-lock techniques acquire another value. They permit you to attack your opponent's body structure directly, doing damage to their ability to fight you. This is a huge advantage. A drunk man may not feel the pain of a dislocated elbow – but no matter how he tries, that arm won't work for him when he wants to punch you.

It follows from this that any serious jointlock technique should also be able to be pushed farther to make it a *joint-destruction* technique. Any jointlock which relies entirely on pain to be effective is of limited value. For the technique to really be effective, you must be able to use it to put the joint out of commission for the duration of the fight.

It is crucial to remember this, because the pain of joint lock techniques affects different people in different ways. I have personally met a number of people who feel very little pain at all from these techniques. They all have acknowledged that they could tell the joint was under stress, and all agreed that if I applied enough pressure to damage the joint it would almost certainly hurt them badly – but I have never tested that assertion. (I should also add I have met a larger number of people who are so powerfully affected by these joint-locks that they will do almost anything to avoid even the beginning of the lock...)

Understand: no joint-lock is secure until it is fully in place, with the opponent off-balanced. Even then, it is possible for an opponent to get used to the level of pain you are applying. It is advisable to vary the pain if you're trying to move or control an opponent. Relax the hold a little when they cooperate, and bring it on more firmly when they show even the slightest sign of resistance or evasion.

Finally: please take care in training. Observe all safety rules, and pay attention to your partner's responses. Applied too strongly, these joint lock techniques cause devastating damage which will almost certainly require surgery for proper repair, and will not recover properly for many months – if ever.

NOTES ON NAMING CONVENTIONS:

Some of these techniques have widely shared names. *Ude garami, ude gatame, kote gaeshi* and *kote mawashi* are fairly common. At the other end of the spectrum, things like *yoko te kubi hishigi* and *tenkai kote hineri* get different names across different styles and systems, including aikido. It really doesn't help.

I've selected the names that suited me, from my own background and instructors. The names more or less reflect what the lock is meant to do, which is a convention I appreciate. You will almost certainly find that some of these names aren't applicable to whichever system you happen to be practising. Use the names that your instructor prefers. It's as simple as that.

The translations are even looser. *Kote gaeshi*, for example, is a widely used term and it generally gets translated as 'outward wrist twist'. The problem with that translation is that 'kote' is Japanese for 'forearm' ('Ko' meaning 'small', 'te' meaning hand – but 'te' in Japanese also referring to pretty much everything between fingertips and shoulder.). 'Wrist' is translated as 'te kubi', meaning 'neck of the hand'. Worse still, 'gaeshi' translates as 'hold' or 'counter'. Worst of all, while 'mawashi'as a verb means 'turn' or rotate, as a noun it specifically means that horrible belt the Sumo wrestlers wear. I've done my best to offer half-sensible English translations, but as always, you should work with the vocabulary your instructor, your dojo and your school prefer.

Remember also that the versions of the locks presented here are relatively simple. There are many variations on each lock, some of which appear quite different to what is shown here. Again: work with your instructor and your dojo.

Three joint-lock situations:

Joint-lock techniques are core ju jutsu, and have many applications. For ease of reading and memory, I have broken up these techniques by situation. The first section is dedicated to *standing joint-locks*: where your opponent and yourself are both on your feet. The objective of these locks is to control the opponent, or take them to the ground, or at worst to destroy their ability to use the locked joint to fight.

The second section is about *joint-locks as ground restraints*. In this situation, you are assumed to have put your opponent on the ground. For the safety of yourself, onlookers, and even your opponent you want to maintain control over them without necessarily doing the kind of damage that would make it impossible for them to get up and keep fighting. In this situation, you (tori) are assumed to be standing, or at least in a position which allows you to get to your feet swiftly if need be, while your opponent (uke) is on the ground, restrained by the joint-lock. In such cases, your opponent will usually be on their belly or their side, to make counter-attacking difficult.

The third section covers common *jointlocks used on the ground during ground-fighting*. In this case both you and your opponent are assumed to be on the ground. These locks are most commonly used in a sporting context. As far as personal defense goes, it's almost always better to be on your feet than it is to be engaged with your opponent on the ground. It's easier to see what's around you, easier to handle new threats – and easier to run away if that becomes necessary. Being able to fight on the ground is vitally important, but it's even more important to understand when fighting on the ground is a good idea... and when it's not.

PLEASE NOTE:
There is a truly amazing array of variations on all these locks. The versions described and illustrated here are not meant to be the best or most useful. Very simply, in my experience they are among the most common versions taught as a means of introducing the joint-locks. That's all.

Furthermore, the locks themselves are described and illustrated in a static fashion. Applying a lock isn't usually difficult. The real trick is getting yourself and your opponent into a position that makes it possible for you to apply the lock. That's where the real skill comes in, and for each of these locking techniques there are dozens and dozens of ways that might let you achieve them. There are also dozens and dozens of different attacks that you might be responding to. The locks, as depicted here, are simply basic techniques. You can use this book to help remember and identify them. But learning to actually use them? Yes. As usual: a dojo, an instructor, and plenty of training partners.

Section one: Standing joint lock techniques
(Both uke and tori are on their feet.)

There are three possible goals for jointlocks from this situation. If it is feasible, you can try for a jointlock to control your opponent with pain, and by putting them in a structurally weak position. If matters are too far along for that, jointlocks may be used to do immediate structural damage, making it very difficult for your opponent to fight you effectively. Jointlocks may also be used to take an opponent to the ground to make them more vulnerable and easy to control.

Whatever your goal, getting a jointlock from the standing position requires speed, accuracy, and complete commitment. If you are hesitant or undecided about taking the necessary grip and applying the jointlock immediately and powerfully, your opponent will definitely escape the technique and probably harm you in the process. Jointlocks might be "soft" techniques in that you can apply them without immediately harming the opponent – but an indecisively applied jointlock is just as useless as a weak, indecisive punch.

When you set out to punch someone, you are aiming to bring your full power to bear against a vulnerable part of their body. Your approach to jointlocks must be exactly the same, or the techniques will be useless. This simple fact makes practicing jointlocks crucial. If you don't practice them as frequently and as routinely as you do your punches and kicks, you won't have the control you need to use them safely.

Watch your opponent carefully during the first phase of possible conflict. Jointlocks are most likely to be effective when your opponent isn't prepared for them – when they've thrown a committed attack early in the piece, or when they're reaching to grab, or when they're simply off-guard, busy yelling at you.

The other opportunity comes after you've destabilized your opponent by striking them or other means. If you can combine striking with grappling and jointlocks, you have a great advantage over most opponents.

Armpit hold – Waki gatame

Basic technique: As a straight armlock, applying pressure to hyperextend the elbow, tori throws their left elbow over uke's right upper arm. Tori grips uke's right wrist in their right hand, raising uke's right arm and keeping the arm extended. Tori's left hand takes a grip on uke's right forearm, with tori's forearm parallel and outside uke's forearm. This places tori's elbow higher up on uke's forearm. Tori finishes the technique by levering up and out on uke's hand and wrist while trapping uke's upper arm against tori's torso with tori's left elbow. Tori must use a wide, low stance to keep uke bent forward at the waist, preventing escape.

Effectiveness: Mixed. As a standing lock, this version of *waki gatame* is not particularly useful as it is difficult to keep uke in precisely the right place. However it is relatively easy to get into the basic left-arm-over position for *waki gatame*, and it works very well indeed as a means of taking the opponent all the way to the ground. Simply keeping the arm extended and sitting or falling to the ground will bring uke down with you, and leave you in a dominant, controlling position on the ground. It is dangerously easy to destroy the elbow joint with this takedown technique, and it is banned in judo competition.

Common problems:
- Uke's elbow must be kept at exactly the right angle for tori to get damaging pressure on it. It must be positioned so that bending the elbow would move it away from tori's body, not towards. Begin with uke's thumb down, back of the hand facing out. Roll the arm so the thumb moves inwards, then upwards. The joints will lock somewhere around the point where the thumb is approaching vertical. Keep it there. The elbow is vulnerable to this lock now.
- Tori's stance must be wide and low to keep uke's shoulder down, and ensure that uke doesn't just bend their arm and escape.

Notes: If instead of trying to trap and hyperextend the elbow, tori puts their left elbow on uke's right shoulder while keeping uke's arm extended, it is possible to threaten the shoulder joint with dislocation. This is done by keeping uke's shoulder trapped with tori's elbow, while pushing uke's extended right hand forwards, over uke's face and head.

Arm entanglement – *Ude garami*

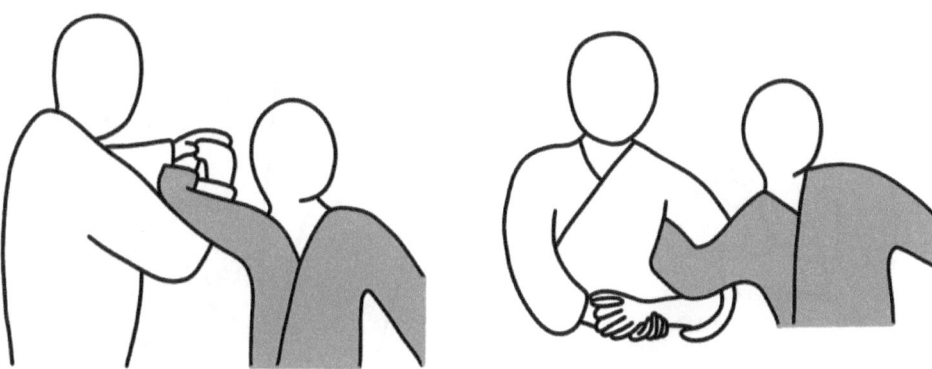

Basic technique: Despite the name, this is a shoulder dislocation technique. Tori stands facing the opposite direction to uke. Uke's right arm is raised to shoulder level, bent at the elbow so the hand points up, and towards uke's head. Tori's right arm is positioned with the forearm behind uke's upper right arm, and right hand gripping uke's right hand on the inside of the wrist. Tori's left hand reaches across to help anchor the grip on uke's right wrist. The technique is completed by tori pushing forward and down with both hands, levering uke's right hand backwards until either uke falls, or the shoulder dislocates as the right arm goes over backwards.

Effectiveness: Limited value as a standing control technique. You can bend the opponent back and keep them off balance, but it is difficult to maintain control. However as a dislocation technique or a hard takedown, *ude garami* is excellent.

Common problems:
- The 'figure four' position must be maintained. If uke straightens their right elbow, the lock will be lost.
- You must intercept uke's arm while their hand is level with their head, or farther back. If you block or catch the hand when it has begun to descend, it is very hard to overcome the strength of uke's arm to apply the technique. However if the hand is back, the arm is weak and easily manipulated.

Notes: There are at least three other versions of this lock done in the standing position, all offering more value as genuine control techniques. One is illustrated above, with tori and uke's arm held low, at waist level. Tori exerts pressure and applies control by facing the same direction as uke, with uke's right arm tucked behind tori's back. Tori's two hands lock in front, left arm under uke's elbow. As tori lifts with their hands, pushes forward with their hips and leans back with the upper body, uke's arm is levered backwards putting sufficient strain on the shoulder to dislocate it easily.

Reverse arm entanglement – *Ushiro ude garami*

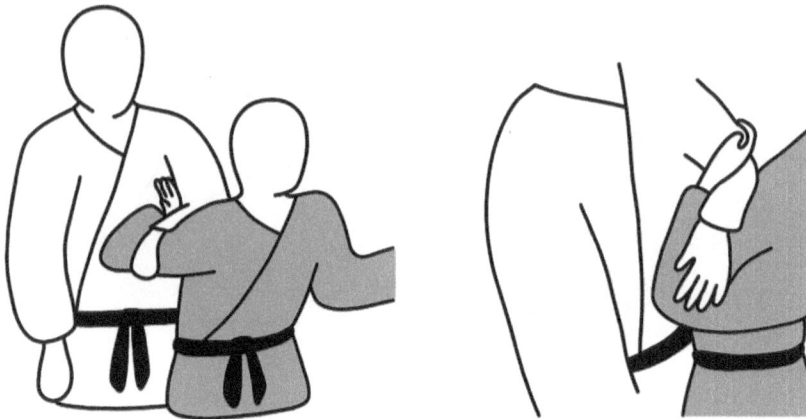

Basic technique: Tori is behind uke. Uke's right arm is behind their back, bent at the elbow so the forearm is approximately horizontal across uke's back. Tori's left arm threads under uke's right forearm, and tori's left hand clasps uke's upper right arm a little above the elbow. Tori's right hand controls uke's right shoulder or uke's throat, forcing uke to stand upright. The technique is completed by tori lifting uke's right hand both outward from their back, and upward towards their shoulder. Note the illustration does not show tori gripping throat, hair, collar or shoulder with the right hand. This is to allow detail of the left hand overlock to show.

Effectiveness: *Ushiro ude garami* is also known as a 'hammerlock', and is a widely used police come-along hold. While it's not the most effective as far as actual joint-locks go, positionally it is excellent. If tori maintains control over uke's arm and keeps uke upright with the shoulder or throat hold, it is difficult for uke to resist or counter attack, and tori can march uke off the premises with relative ease.

Common problems:
- Simply pushing uke's hand higher behind their back will not affect flexible people. You must pull the hand outwards as well to cause pain and eventual dislocation.
- Left hand on right arm for this technique.
- Keep uke upright. If they can bend forward they can escape the pain, and slip the lock.

Notes:
- Done during ground-fighting, this technique is widely known as a *kimura*, a term popularized by the Brazilian jujitsu movement.
- This lock is extremely painful to persons with heavily developed shoulder muscles if they have not worked to ensure good flexibility. Weightlifters in particular are vulnerable here. The simple act of putting their wrist behind their back can cause such people tremendous pain. Be careful in training.

Straight armlock – *Ude gatame*

Basic technique: Tori stands on uke's right, both facing forward. Tori's left arm wraps over and around uke's right arm. Tori's right hand hold's uke's right hand at the wrist. Uke's palm is upard, but tori uses their right hand grip to roll the wrist outward, moving the thumb downward so the palm faces tori. Tori completes the technique by grasping their own right wrist with their left hand. Tori pulls down and twists uke's right arm to straighten the elbow, and leans back to position uke's right elbow over tori's left forearm. Tori's left forearm acts as a fulcrum, placing great stress on the elbow as tori tightens the grip and leans back.

Effectiveness: High. There are many versions of this lock. Simply, the arm is straightened and a fulcrum is placed behind the elbow so that tori can apply pressure at the wrist and – if necessary – hyperextend uke's elbow, doing tremendous damage to the joint. The lock is very painful. Different versions can be used as restraints or come-along techniques, and all of them permit tori to destroy the elbow if necessary.

Common problems:
- Uke's arm must be properly extended
- The fulcrum must be placed against the elbow accurately, allowing the lever-action of the grip to cause pain and threaten damage. If the fulcrum is too high or too low, the lock will not work.

Uses: *Ude gatame* is a highly versatile lock. It can be a come-along, or a static restraint. It can be used to keep an opponent on the ground after you throw them. It can also be used to drive uke into a throw, by using the pain and leverage of the technique. An example of this is the throw *kata guruma*, which becomes devastatingly powerful if uke is thrown with their arm locked in this technique.

Notes: Two other common variations are depicted above. In one, uke's arm is levered down across tori's arm while tori reaches across and locks onto uke's collar, or even slides the hand behind uke's neck. In the other, uke's arm is levered across tori's shoulders from above, while tori reaches around uke's back with the other hand to control tori's opposite arm. Both are effective come-along techniques. There are many other useful versions of this lock.

Outwards forearm twist – *Kote gaeshi*

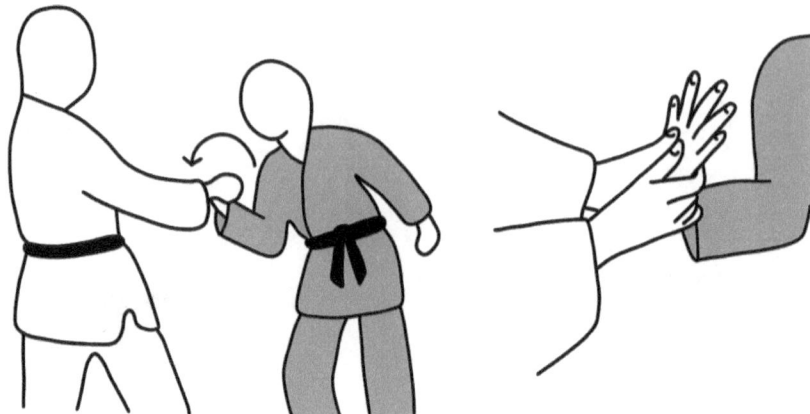

Basic technique: Tori faces uke, on the left (from tori's view) of uke's centreline. Tori holds uke's right hand with both hands. Uke's hand is bent at the wrist, fingers upward, palm facing uke. Tori's grip is specific: the fingers of the left hand hook around the base of uke's right thumb, while the thumb of the left hand pushes strongly against the first knuckles of the index and middle finger. Tori's right fingers curl around the muscles of the outer edge of uke's right palm, while tori's right thumb presses strongly against the first knuckle of uke's third finger. Tori pushes forward with the thumbs to bend uke's hand, and twists outward – to tori's left – to increase stress on the wrist. To finish the technique, tori maintains both forward and twisting pressure while taking a single step towards uke's right shoulder. The pain and stress on uke's wrist should force uke into a fall to their right.

Effectiveness: Moderate. All you can do with this is throw uke to the ground or destroy the wrist joint. If you simply apply pressure, uke merely has to shift their body to release the pressure. Further: if you do not apply the pressure swiftly and sharply, uke can easily reach across with their other hand to brace, disarming the technique. However if you do act swiftly and sharply, this technique works well – either to put your opponent down, or destroy the function of their wrist.

Common problems:
- Will not immobilise a standing opponent. Must be used as a takedown or a joint-damaging technique.
- Keep your hands low, at hip level. If you let your hands rise, you give your opponent much more 'play' in the technique and they are likely to escape.
- Do not rely on hand strength to finish the technique. Keep your hands low, at hip level, and step in to commit your body weight into the takedown. In this fashion a smaller person can put a much larger and stronger person on the ground if the technique is quickly and aggressively applied.

Notes: Untrained people don't automatically fall to the ground to escape moderate pain. Many of them will flail around and struggle violently. You must commit strongly to this technique to force their body to respond instantly and thoughtlessly to the pain – and you must be prepared to do real damage to the joint if necessary. This is important. Your training partners will co-operate to a degree to escape the pain. This is the logical response of a trained person. A startled, untrained opponent will struggle to stay upright, and you must overwhelm their fear with pain if you want them to fall.

Wrist crush – *Te kubi hishigi*

Basic technique: Tori and uke are side by side, with uke on tori's left, both facing forward. Uke's right arm is bent at the elbow, the upper arm raised to about 45 degrees from vertical. Tori's left arm tucks under and behind uke's right arm, and both of tori's hands are engaged with uke's right hand. Uke's right hand is folded strongly down, as if tori is trying to press uke's the pads of uke's fingers against uke's forearm. Tori's thumbs may be against uke's palm, or if uke is flexible, may pass around the upper surface of uke's forearm for added pressure. The lock is applied when tori pulls strongly against the first knuckles of uke's right hand, bending the wrist powerfully and trapping uke's right elbow in the space between tori's left upper arm and torso.

Effectiveness: High, once the lock is fully in place. With both hands available to compress uke's wrist joint, it is easy to apply a great deal of pain. If pain isn't enough to control the opponent, it isn't difficult to pull back sharply on their hand, compressing their forearm into your elbow, and badly damaging the wrist joint.

Common problems:
- If uke is unusually flexible, it may be difficult to apply sufficient compression to cause pain
- Uke's elbow must be tucked firmly into the gap under tori's armpit, and trapped against tori's body, otherwise uke can step forward and jerk the elbow up, out of compression, and escape the lock.

Uses: This is a very common police come-along hold. It becomes even more brutally painful and effective if tori twists uke's trapped right hand, gripping all of uke's fingers in tori's left so that the fingers are horizontal to the ground, pointing across tori's body. This turns the hold into a version of *yoko te kubi hishigi*, and it is excruciating. Further, since it can be done with the left hand alone it leaves tori's right hand free to perform other tasks – using a phone, for example, or opening doors.

Side wrist crush – *Yoko te kubi hishigi*

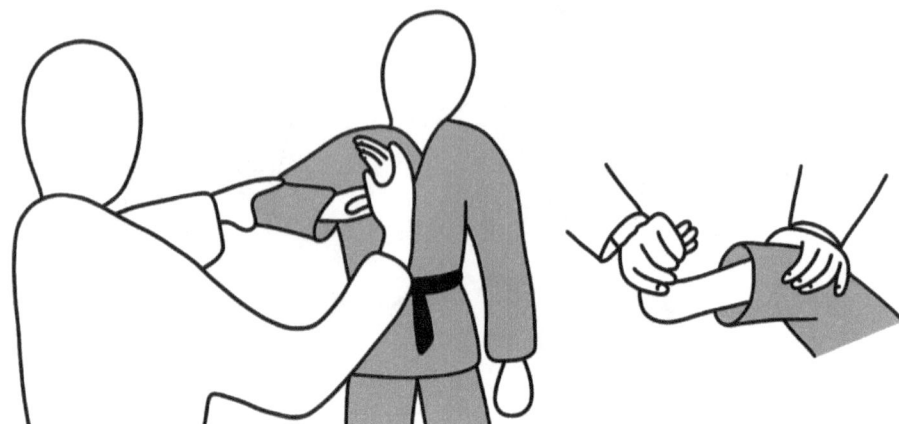

Basic technique: Standing to uke's right, tori uses the left hand to brace the back of uke's right elbow. Tori's right hand grabs all of uke's fingers, with tori's thumb across uke's palm. Tori raises uke's right arm to horizontal, ensuring uke's elbow is bent. To finish the technique, tori bends uke's right wrist until it locks, then uses the grip on the fingers to rotate the hand upwards, bringing the uke's fingertips towards uke's face until uke sinks down to avoid the pressure.

Effectiveness: Very high. The version shown and described here is the least effective, but the easiest to describe and to clearly depict. The pain from this jointlock is immense, and it requires little extra pressure in the twist of the wrist to do great damage to the wrist joint.

Common problems:
- Both uke's wrist and elbow need to be bent. The angle on the wrist should be as extreme as possible.
- Pain is caused by the rotational action, not by simple compression on the wrist

Uses: Various versions of *yoko te kubi hishigi* are utilised as extremely effective come-along holds. It is also a useful quick-finish technique against a variety of grabbing attacks that may occur early in a conflict.

Notes: As always, the technique must be applied quickly and forcefully, with the understanding that untrained persons may struggle (foolishly) rather than comply with the pain. Full commitment to the technique is important. You should enter it with the understanding that you may have to damage the opponent's wrist if they do not comply with the pain.

Forearm turnover – *Kote mawashi*

Basic technique: Tori grasps uke's hand with both hands, reversing uke's hand so the palm is upward and the thumb points back behind uke. One of tori's hands grips the outer edge of uke's palm on the side of the little finger. The other hand grasps the base of uke's thumb. Both of tori's thumbs apply strong pressure to the back of uke's hand, bending it upward at the wrist. Tori takes a deep step back into *zen kutsu dachi*, pulling sharply on uke's hand to extend and straighten the arm, causing uke to lower their head and bend their body. Direct inward pressure with both of tori's thumbs applies stress and pain to the wrist, keeping uke's head down.

Effectiveness: Limited. The physical action of putting the lock in place and pulling sharply backward will usually bring uke's body over and down, but the pain from this technique is relatively low, and there are many ways for uke to move out of it. Most importantly, it is extremely difficult to extend this technique to the point where it actually damages the wrist and prevents your opponent attacking with the hand. However it is an easy position to reach, and makes a good base from which to move to other techniques.

Common problems:
- Tori must not press with their fingers against the actual wrist joint. This will provide support for the joint and reduce the pain. Tori's thumbs press the back of the hand, while the fingers press in the opposite direction into the palm, forcing the wrist to bend and stressing the joint.
- Tori must remember to draw strongly back on the arm to offbalance uke, and to assume a strong, balanced *zen kutsu dachi*. Simple joint pressure alone is not sufficient for this technique to unbalance and control uke.

Uses: *Kote mawashi* is a good transitional position. Pulling strongly at the arm while applying pressure to the hand will usually cause uke to bend, lining them up for a strong kick to the body or head. It is easy to flow from this position to more effective controlling locks including *ude gatame*, *te kubi hishigi* and *yoko te kubi hishigi*

Forearm twist – Kote hineri

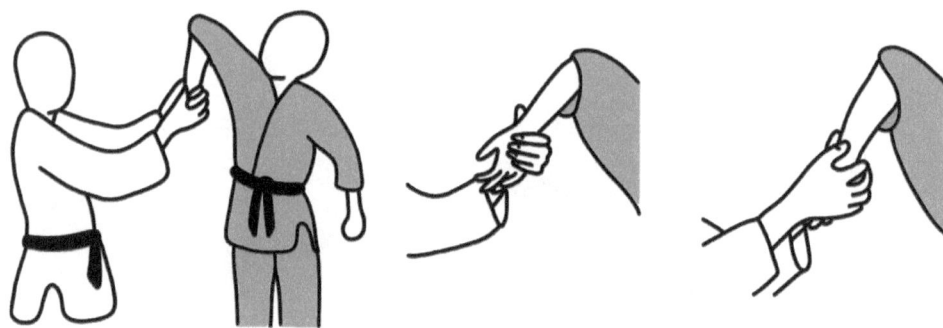

Basic technique: Tori holds uke's right hand with both hands. Tori's left-hand grip is crucial: the fingers wrap around the muscle at the little finger edge of uke's palm, while tori's thumb pushes strongly against the first knuckle of uke's index finger, allowing tori to twist the hand strongly. Tori's right hand clasps uke's palm to support tori's left hand and increase the twist strength. The technique is applied by twisting uke's hand so that the thumb turns inward, under the arm. At the same time, tori uses the hand grip to push uke's elbow up towards uke's head, forcing uke up on their toes.

Effectiveness: Variable. With precision and training, it is possible to use this as a control technique, but it is quite difficult. Uke has considerable freedom of movement, and by turning their body and lowering their elbow they can escape this hold easily. However if *kote hineri* is applied quickly and sharply, it is easy to do terrible damage to the wrist and forearm. If tori holds the grip tightly and keeps uke's hand close to their chest while turning towards or even ducking under uke's armpit, the torsion on the two bones of the forearm causes tremendous pain, and can easily tear tendons and ligaments, even snap the smaller bone.

Common problems:
- Tori should keep the grip close to their own body. The farther out the hold, the more room uke has for movement and potential escape.
- Uke's elbow must be kept high, and pushed towards uke's head. If it is allowed to drop forwards or backwards, uke can easily turn out of the grip and counterattack.

Uses: Limited value as a control technique, but it does lead to several powerful take-downs using stress and pain. Applied quickly and strongly *kote hineri* will effectively destroy the opponent's ability to use the hand and forearm for the forseeable future.

Reverse wrist crush – *Gyaku te kubi hishigi*

Basic technique: Tori stands on uke's right, both facing forward. Tori's left arm passes under uke's right armpit, between the arm and uke's torso. Tori's right hand reaches across and grasps uke's fingers from the first joint on down. Uke's hand is palm outwards, fingers down. Uke's right elbow is trapped in between tori's left arm and tori's torso. The technique is finished by tori closing both hands over uke's right fingers and pulling back strongly, putting stress on the finger joints and the wrist.

Effectiveness: Quite limited. Some people are sensitive to pain in the finger joints. Some, on the other hand, are flexible and the fingers will bend farther than you think. Meanwhile, the stress on the wrist is quite limited due to the natural structure of the body, and this technique causes very little pain. If you want it to work you're likely to be better off concentrating on the fingers.

Common problems:
- Basically not very effective on most people
- Uke's elbow must be properly trapped, or uke can lift it up and walk out of the technique.

Uses: Hyperextension of the fingers (small joint technique) can be useful, but unreliable. This position makes you quite dependent on the pain control which may not work, and finger dislocations – while painful – aren't really enough in terms of structural damage to your opponent to be of great assistance to you.

Notes: This lock is shown largely for the sake of completion. With *yoko te kubi hishigi*, *te kubi hishigi*, and *kote gaeshi*, it represents the four basic directions you can lock up the wrist joints. (Note that *kote hineri* puts more stress on the structure of the forearm rather than the wrist itself.)

Section two: Joint locking techniques as ground restraints

In these techniques, tori is standing, or in a position which allows them to stand quickly and easily. Uke is on the ground, restrained by the joint lock technique.

Having the ability to restrain a person without beating them senseless or destroying all their limbs is useful, especially for people who may find themselves working in the security industry. Joint-locking techniques are particularly useful in this area. Applied properly, a good ground restraint allows tori to maintain their own balance and permits observation of the surroundings, while still maintaining the threat of crippling damage to the restrained person.

Note that last sentence. Just as with any other joint-lock technique, a ground restraint relies on tori's ability to do immediate, devastating damage if uke attempts to resist. There is a mental and emotional element to this idea. It's one thing to put a restraint in place in the dojo, on a trained partner who understands what's happening. It's entirely another to use the same restraint against an angry, injured, maybe drunk or drugged person who doesn't know what's going on.

The only information that such a person has comes from their immediate senses. You must apply the technique correctly so that the pain becomes overwhelming every time they try to do something you don't want. You must use your voice, giving them instructions to make it clear what they must do to avoid the pain. Above all, you must be prepared to do real damage to the restrained person if they continue to present a danger.

Finally: struggling to put a lock onto a person who is thrashing around on the ground is dangerous. These restraints are applied **after** you've effectively subdued your opponent, even if only briefly. Typically, they come after you have thrown someone violently to the ground, disorienting and possibly stunning them – and very possibly after you've put in a few quick strikes to keep them disoriented.

If you cannot readily make a ground restraint work, and your opponent continues to represent a real threat, you may have to consider using your superior position to do enough damage to prevent them doing further harm. Always remember that anything you do may well be evaluated later in a court of law – so appropriate restraint is always correct.

Ground restraint – *Kote hineri*

Basic technique: Uke lies on the ground on their left side. Tori stands over them. Tori's right foot tucks into uke's lower belly to prevent uke moving hips forward or rolling. Tori's left hand grips uke's right hand. Tori's fingers fold over the edge of the little finger side of uke's palm, pressing into the palm. Tori's thumb braces behind the index finger/thumb side of uke's palm. To complete the technique, tori twists uke's hand, bringing the thumb side forward across the palm towards the little finger.

Comments and notes:
- This is a really useful ground restraint. It can be done safely with just one hand if you have the grip properly applied. It is extremely painful. It takes little effort to twist through and do very serious damage to the tendons, ligaments and bones of the wrist and forearm. It is also easy to manipulate the grip and bring uke to their feet under control if uke proves cooperative. And of course, leaving you in an upright condition with one hand fully free is very nice.
- Be sure to step over uke's body, and kick back in tightly to the torso. Just like the standing *kote hineri*, uke can try to twist and push their shoulder forward to escape – but all you have to do is keep stress on the wrist, keep the arm from bending too far at the shoulder, and prevent uke rolling or shifting their hips with your front foot.
- This is also an easy ground-lock to achieve from most throwing techniques if you retain control of the arm.

Straight armlock ground restraint #1 – *Ude gatame*

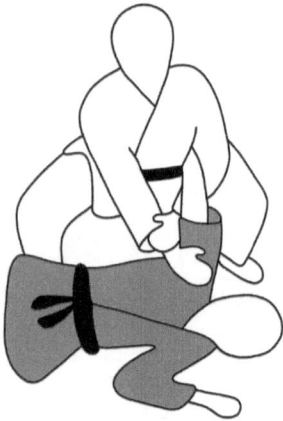

Basic technique: From a wide, low stance, tori slides their left arm under uke's right, as uke lies on the ground on their left side. Tori ensures uke's right hand is trapped up behind tori's upper arm, palm upwards. Tori's left forearm passes directly under uke's right elbow. Tori's right hand sits on top of uke's right shoulder. Tori's left hand grips tori's right forearm. Tori leans back and straightens their arms to put tension into the armlock, applying pressure with tori's left forearm against the back of uke's right elbow. If tori continues to lean back and push up into a standing position, they can apply enough pressure to hyperextend uke's right elbow, tearing it apart. Tori should continue to apply sufficient pain to keep uke compliant.

Comments and notes:
- Uke's right arm must be kept straight. Uke must not be allowed to bend the arm. Use the pain of the lock to roll uke forward, away from you, and lift their torso slightly to prevent them kicking.
- Holding this position for an extended time is difficult, owing to the depth of the stance needed.
- Transitioning to a standing position can be done if uke is compliant. Keep the lock on, and move carefully towards uke's feet, allowing uke to get their balance and stand. Maintain the lock, and ensure that uke understands the consequences of any attempt at resistance.

Straight armlock ground restraint #2 – *Ude gatame*

Basic technique: Uke is on the ground lying on their left side. Tori holds uke's right hand with their own right hand. Uke's palm faces away from tori. Tori steps over uke's head with the left leg, tucking their left heel under uke's throat. Tori kicks their right foot under uke's ribs and leans into the right leg, angling the knee forward. With the right hand controlling uke's right hand, tori braces uke's extended right arm against tori's right shin below the knee. As tori pulls against uke's right hand, uke's elbow will be hyperextended against tori's shin. Tori must keep the left foot in place to prevent uke tucking forward to take pressure off the elbow. Tori must also lean into the right knee so uke can't shift their hips enough to relieve pressure. The hold works best if tori's knee and shin force uke to roll towards their left, putting them closer to a face-down position. If uke attempts to resist, it is easy for tori to pull back on uke's right hand, tearing apart uke's right elbow against tori's right shin.

Comments and notes:
- This hold down allows for a comfortable standing position, and is easy to maintain.
- Moving uke to a standing position from this hold is difficult. It is better for tori to withdraw their left foot and roll uke onto their belly using the leverage of the armlock, change to something like *ushiro ude garami*, and stand them up that way if necessary.
- Uke's arm must be kept straight, and it is vital that tori maintains control over the right wrist so that uke cannot roll the arm to a position where the elbow is no longer threatened.
- Don't forget to trap uke's head with the left heel under the throat from the front. Without that, uke can simply move around on the ground to escape the lock.
- It is vital that uke's arm is trapped below tori's knee, against the shin, with the shin angled forward to keep the elbow from slipping up and over.

Hanging wrist crush ground restraint – *Te kubi hishigi*

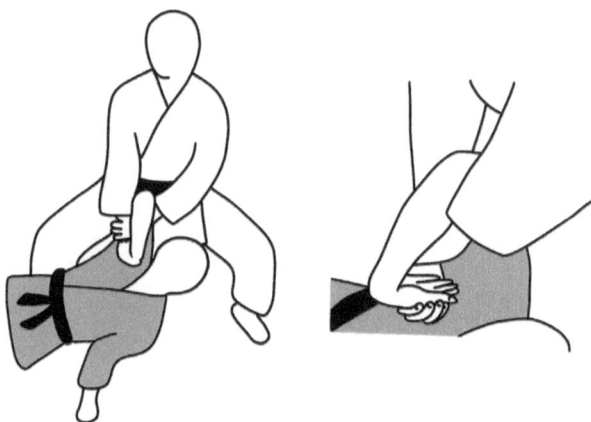

Basic technique: Uke's right arm is bent like a chicken-wing, with the back of uke's right hand near their armpit. Tori is in a wide, low stance above uke. Tori's right hand cups the back of uke's right hand close to the first knuckles, forcing uke's right hand into a painfully bent position. Tori's fingers curl around uke's hand, gripping it in place and locking it in position with tori's thumb over the palm. With the left hand, tori reaches under uke's right elbow and locks their grip onto their own right wrist. Keeping uke's elbow pointed upward and close to tori's own body, tori completes the technique by raising their stance, pushing up with hips and legs. As tori rises, pressure on uke's bent right hand increases until uke's weight hangs from it. This is extremely painful. Tori should lift uke into a position where uke is struggling to support themselves with their other hand. Tori must not allow uke to get their feet under them. If uke attempts to struggle or escape, tori can stand quickly to use uke's weight to destroy the right wrist.

Comments and notes:
- Tori's left hand grasps tori's own right wrist to lock and anchor the technique. It is crucial that tori's left arm should not supply any support to uke's elbow when tori is lifting to put the technique in place. All of uke's upper body weight must be focused through the bent wrist.
- Uke must not be permitted to rest comfortably on the ground, or there is a possibility they might try to kick. Tori must keep uke suspended, partially supported by their own left hand, with the threat of tearing the wrist joint clearly present.
- It is easy to pick uke up to a standing position from this technique, if it becomes necessary to walk them away. Tori's right hand maintains the wrist crush, but tori slides the left hand around uke's neck to grasp throat or collar. Tori now tucks uke's elbow tightly into tori's body, and moves slowly and gently towards uke's feet. Pressure on the trapped right hand and the throat grip plus appropriate verbal instruction will move uke to get their feet under them and transition to a standing position. Tori maintains control with the right hand wrist crush and the potential strangle. If uke attempts to struggle or escape, the throat and wrist control make a foot sweep takedown simple, and tori can move back to the original control position.

Double leg tie ground restraint

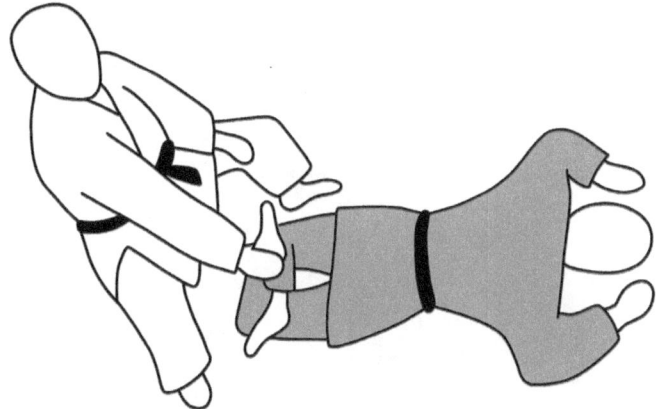

Basic technique: Uke is on the ground, face town. Tori tucks one of uke's ankles into the back of the opposite knee, then folds that leg up, trapping the ankle. From here, tori need only apply strong pressure to the foot of the entrapping leg to cause excruciating pain to the knee joint. If tori applies enough body weight to the foot of the entrapping leg, it is possible to separate and rupture the knee entirely.

Comments and notes:
- Not easily done by tori while standing. You can try applying weight to the foot of the entrapping leg with your own foot, but it's difficult to keep your balance, and to apply enough weight without accidentally going too far. Most efficient means of doing this hold-down probably calls for tori to kneel, giving up the advantage of quick mobility.
- It isn't easy to get uke into this position. Legs are strong. Unless uke is already pretty thoroughly stunned or damaged, they can resist this technique quite effectively before it comes on.
- Having said that – using *ashi gatame* to turn uke on their belly gives you control over one leg, and pain compliance may allow you to achieve the leg trap after that.
- Applying full strength to this lock will very thoroughly destroy the ligaments and tendons around the knee joint.

Spine lock ground restraint

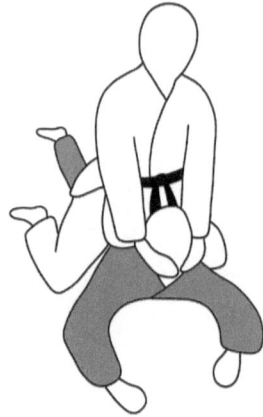

Basic technique: Uke is face down on the ground. Tori sits on uke's hips or lower back, facing uke's head. Using both hands, tori pulls back uke's head using grips to sensitive or vulnerable areas such as the nerves under the jaw, the eyes, ears, or nose. Once the head is lifted and pulled back to the limits of spinal movement it becomes impossible for uke to reach back, and pain compliance can be used to prevent efforts at rolling.

Comments and notes:
- The value of most jointlock restraints is increased by the fact that if uke struggles, you can destroy or damage the joint to reduce uke's ability to fight. Breaking uke's spine, however, is almost certainly going to cause you legal problems.
- This technique works quite well once you've got uke's spine arched and their head pulled up and back, because it overextends the muscles that uke needs to pull everything back into line. But if you let uke get their head down, you'll be fighting against all those muscles at their strongest, and if uke is significantly larger or stronger than you, you're going to have a problem.
- The seated posture is comfortable, but of course you're subject to the usual vulnerabilities of being on the ground.
- How long are you really prepared to sit there holding their head locked back like that?
- The good news is that if you decide to just shut down the whole thing, you can transition to *hadaka jime* easily from here, and render uke unconscious.

Leg entanglement ground restraint – *Ashi garami*

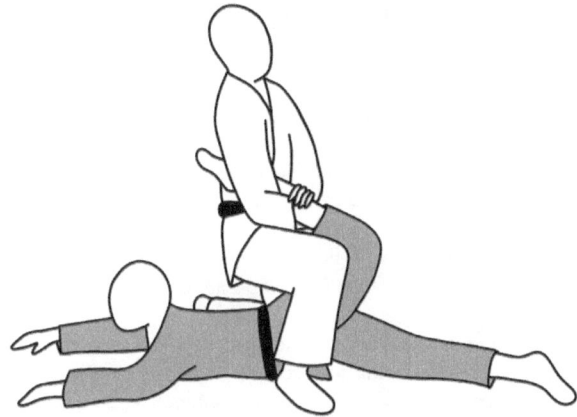

Basic technique: Uke is face down on the ground. Tori kneels over uke with their right foot outside uke's lower left back. Tori has uke's left ankle tucked into tori's right armpit. Tori's right forearm passes under uke's left calf, and tori's right hand locks onto tori's left forearm, Tori's left hand is braced against uke's right shin. To complete the technique, tori tightens the grip and leans back so the blade of tori's right forearm pressures the lower gastrocnemius muscle and tibial nerve, while uke's right foot is levered in the opposite direction, putting stress on the ankle joint.

Comments and notes:
- Not as difficult to enter as you might think. Trapping the leg with this basic technique from a poorly delivered front kick is reasonably simple, and twisting the trapped leg to overthrow the unbalanced uke is also simple. Once uke is on the ground, it's just a matter of using the pain of the lock to control them while you step over into position.
- Getting enough leverage on the ankle to do real damage can be difficult.
- The kneeling position is comfortable for tori, and allows good observation of the surroundings. The strong arch of the back and the leverage on the leg is extremely unpleasant for uke.
- It isn't difficult to transition from this to the double-leg tie if you feel the need to put uke's knee in serious danger.
- It is also possible to stand up, anchoring uke with one foot. This will stretch uke, and stress the spine.
- If the spine is properly bent, it is very difficult for uke to kick back and up with the free foot.
- Don't overdo the spine stretch. There's an old wrestling version of this hold with both legs trapped under the arms. It's called 'The Boston Crab', and because tori can bring their full bodyweight to bear by simply sitting back and down, it's a potential spine-destroyer. You don't want that.

Section three:
Joint lock techniques for ground-fighting

In this situation, both uke and tori are on the ground, struggling for control or dominance. This is where BJJ systems are especially dominant – but in general, defensive ju jutsu prefers to avoid this. When you're on the ground fully engaged with one opponent, it's far too easy for one of their allies unknown to you to come up and kick you in the back of the head. Remaining on your feet, mobile and alert is very much the safer situation unless you are completely sure your opponent has no help at hand.

Nevertheless, it's important to acknowledge that you can be taken to the ground against your will, or simply lose your footing, and thus may be forced into this kind of fight. Only a fool would insist it is impossible for them to be drawn into a ground fight, and no system of defensive martial arts is complete without a comprehensive understanding of the ground game, and at least a basic set of techniques to work with.

These jointlocks are more commonly used by ju jutsu in the sporting context. Nevertheless, they remain effective. As always, the ability to destroy your opponent's physical structure goes a long way towards shutting down their capacity to do you harm. Joint lock techniques lead to the destruction of the enemy's joints if necessary – and you must bear this in mind if you find yourself needing to use these.

Scarf entanglement – *Kesa garami*

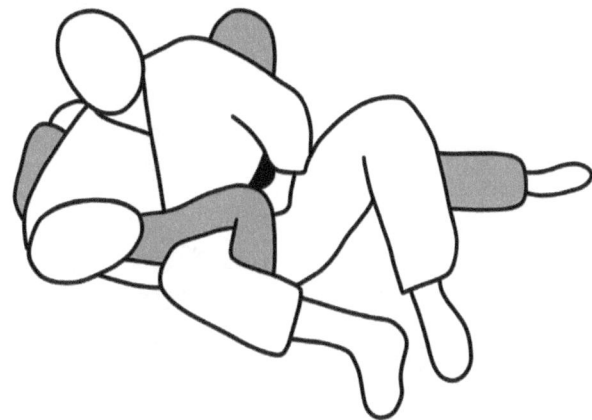

Basic technique: This hold usually comes from *kesa gatame*. Uke is on the floor, on their back. Tori sits with their right hip snugly against uke's ribs, legs splayed for stability. Tori places their weight on uke's upper body and wraps uke's head and neck tightly into tori's chest. Tori controls uke's head and neck with their right arm, but instead of wrapping uke's arm around tori's waist, tori tucks uke's right hand back under tori's right calf and locks it in place by bending their right leg. The lock is completed by tori bending the right leg more, and pushing up with their hips, leading to a dislocation of the shoulder if necessary.

Effectiveness: High. Once this is locked in, there's not a whole lot uke can do except possibly scream. It's a good position for tori to negotiate from as well. But of course, if uke has help this posture is as vulnerable as any other ground position.

Common problems:
- Tori must remember to bend the right leg in order to trap uke's right hand. If uke can straighten the arm, the lock is gone and escape becomes possible.

Notes:
- If uke does straighten the arm, of course, another variation of the hold comes into play. With uke's right arm straight, tori can place their right thigh under uke's elbow as a fulcrum. Tori can then use their left foot or left leg as a lever against uke's arm, applying a vicious straight armlock against uke's right elbow.
- Despite the fact that the straight armlock version operates against the elbow and the bent arm version dislocates the shoulder – both of these variations are considered *kesa garami*. Go figure, eh?

Grounded figure four arm entanglement – Ude garami

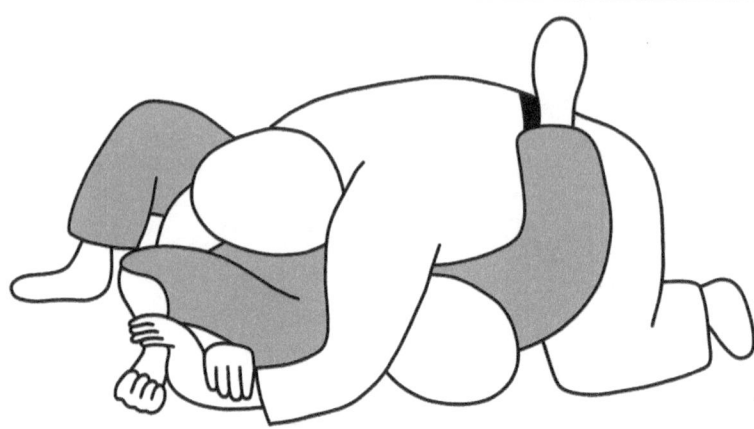

Basic technique: Tori lies over uke's chest. Tori's left hand restrains uke's left wrist, rotating it strongly outward (away from tori.) Tori's right hand feeds under uke's left elbow and grasps tori's left wrist. To complete the technique, tori levers upward on uke's left elbow, applying torque and stress to uke's left shoulder.

Effectiveness: Not great. In 1925, the Kodokan Judo governing body ruled that the only *kansetsu waza* that could be used in competition must be "applied to the elbow-joint". That has been interpreted to mean that the source of the action must be the elbow, even if the pain occurs elsewhere. So – this version of *ude garami* exists because judoka have been hair-splitting their own rules and they wanted to keep at least some kind of attack on the shoulder, even if it was a limited one.

Common problems:
- Remember to rotate the wrist out, not in. Rotating it in gives uke a bit more breathing room.

Notes:
- Plenty of people are flexible enough that lifting their elbow from that position doesn't actually cause much pain. Also, it's difficult to dislocate the shoulder from here in any case.

Cross armlock – *Juji gatame*

Basic technique: Uke is on the ground on their back. Tori sits with their hips as close as possible to uke's torso on uke's right side, holding strongly to uke's right arm. Tori's left leg goes over uke, above the trapped right arm. To enter the technique, tori draws up strongly on uke's right arm. Tori puts their right leg over uke's torso, ideally winding it under uke's left arm and crossing their right ankle over their left ankle to lock the legs in position. Keeping a tight grip on uke's right hand, tori leans back using body weight to extend uke's right arm until the elbow is at full extension. Tori finishes by levering uke's elbow across tori's upper thigh until either uke submits, or the elbow is ruptured.

Effectiveness: High. If the opponent has no allies on site, this is an excellent follow-up to a throw. It can be entered quickly, and once it's locked in place it's very easy to hold for lengthy periods of time. And of course, at any time you can raise your hips and lever the trapped arm to destroy the elbow.

Common problems:
- Ensure your backside is strongly in contact with uke's torso. You want to be as close as possible for maximum leverage on the arm. A significant gap between your body and theirs will make it possible for uke to bend their elbow and resist the technique.
- Do cross your ankles, and ensure that you cross the ankle farther down uke's torso over the one nearer uke's head – otherwise uke can use their left arm to simply throw your uppermost leg over their head and sit up to escape the lock.

Uses: *Ude hishigi juji gatame* (the full formal name of this technique) is absolutely great if you're quite sure the other person has nobody with them. Done correctly, this hold will allow a relatively small person to restrain (or very badly damage) a much larger and potentially stronger person. However it still requires complete commitment, especially if you're dealing with a larger, stronger person and under circumstances where the opponent has allies any ground-based hold has limited value.

Armpit hold – *Waki gatame*

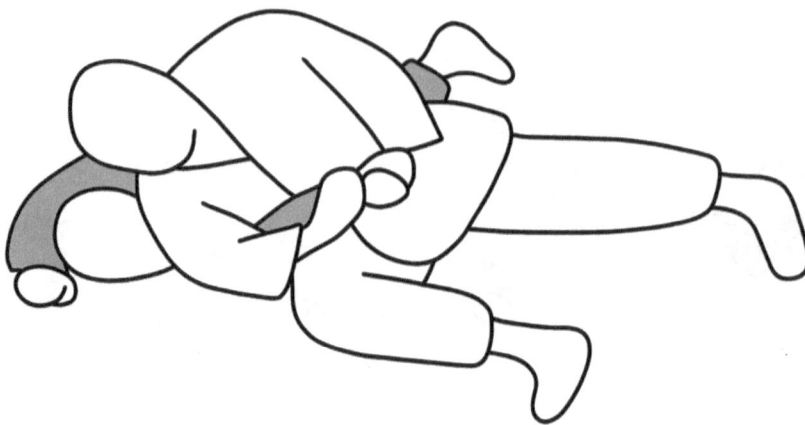

Basic technique: Uke is face down. Tori is on uke's left, facing uke's head end, pressed tight to uke's torso with uke's left arm stretched across tori's midsection. Both tori's hands restrain uke's left wrist. Tori leans into uke's shoulder joint to prevent uke rolling. The technique is completed by tori turning uke's wrist so the point of the elbow is pressed to tori's middle, and tori then pulls back on the wrist to hyperextend the elbow.

Effectiveness: Moderate. Largely a sporting technique. Note that this hold is another victim of hair-splitting. Uke's arm often bends to wrap around tori's middle – but tori still gets a submission by lifting the wrist and leaning into the shoulder joint. This applies a shoulder dislocation – but it still gets by Kodokan rules because technically tori is manipulating the elbow, not the shoulder.

Common problems:
- If uke can bend their arm around tori's middle, uke can quickly roll over the left shoulder to escape – unless tori rapidly transitions to the shoulder dislocation.

Notes:
- The position of the arm for the shoulder dislocation is much the same as that of the *omoplata*.
- Simple superiority of leverage due to tori's weight on uke's restrained shoulder will usually allow this technique to be used to hold an untrained person indefinitely.

Grounded shoulder lock – *Gyaku ude garami/Ushiro ude garami/Kimura*

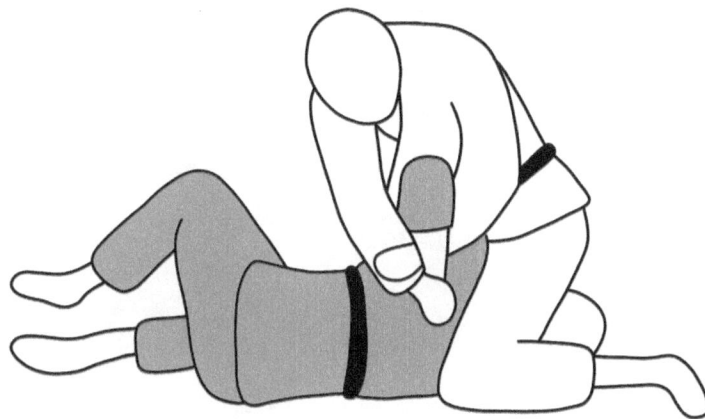

Basic technique: There are many ways to do a 'kimura', which is simply a bent-arm shoulder lock either behind the body, or in front of it. We've already covered the version from in front (*ude garami*, grounded) so we'll look at a rear version from side mount. Uke lies on their right side. Tori straddles uke's head and shoulders, facing uke's feet. Tori's two hands control uke's left wrist, bringing it behind uke's back. Tori's right hand grips uke's wrist, while tori's left arm snakes under uke's bent left elbow and locks onto tori's right wrist for enhanced leverage. The technique is completed by tori pulling uke's trapped left hand back towards uke's head.

Effectiveness: Still a sporting hold, but fairly effective. The side mount described here gives good control over uke's body, and leaves tori in an excellent position to complete the locking technique by dislocating uke's shoulder if necessary.

Common problems:
- There are many ways to put this lock in place. It is important to remember that more than simply pushing uke's hand up behind their back towards their head, you want to achieve separation – pull the hand out and away from the surface of the back as well to gain maximum effect.

Notes:
- 'Kimura' is the name the Brazilian Jiu Jitsu people give this lock because Kimura Masahiko used it to overcome Helio Gracie in a famous match in 1949. I use the term here because it is increasingly known by that name.

Leg-set reverse armlock – *Omoplata/Ashi gatame*

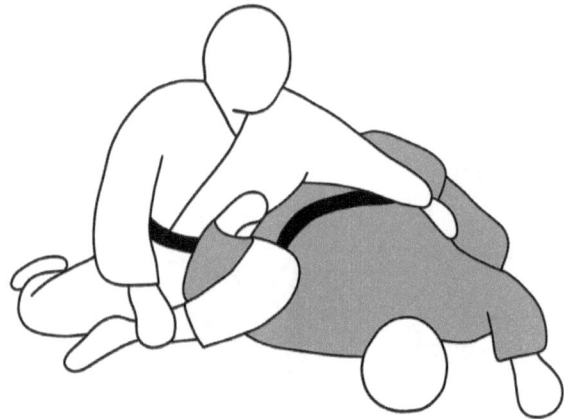

Basic technique: Tori sits next to uke on uke's right, facing towards uke's head. Uke is face down. Tori's left thigh passes over uke's upper right arm. Uke's right arm is bent at the elbow, and the back of uke's hand is braced against tori's lower torso. Tori's left calf and ankle sit horizontally along the ground in front of tori, pointing to tori's right. Tori's right hand grips their left calf to help anchor uke's right arm so uke cannot unbend it. Tori's left hand reaches across uke's torso and takes a solid grip, preventing uke from rolling or twisting to escape. To complete the technique, tori just has to lean forward, letting their torso push uke's right hand up and forward, potentially dislocating the shoulder.

Effectiveness: As a sport hold, the '*omoplata*' (this name has been popularized by the BJJ movement) is a strong finishing technique. Tori is in a powerful, dominant position, able to control uke with the threat of the shoulder dislocation, and by simple superiority of posture. The fact that tori can sit up comfortably and look around makes this a reasonable means of controlling a downed opponent in self defense, always assuming they have no allies. It relies on body weight and the strength of the legs, which means that even a relatively slight person can use this hold to restrain a much larger and more powerful opponent if it is applied correctly.

Common problems:
- Uke's arm must be bent at the elbow, with the forearm raised and braced. If uke can straighten the arm, they can roll to slip out as there's no pain or lock any more.
- Tori should keep hips and lower torso close and tight to uke's body and forearm. Too much freedom of action for uke may result in the arm straightening and uke escaping.

Notes: Watch for an attempted forward roll from your opponent as you apply this. While it is less likely in a self-defense situation, the pain on the shoulder may make it almost an instinctive action. For training partners who are taught to roll, it will come easily. Be very careful. If their roll is timed badly or carried out incorrectly, it is very easy to damage uke's shoulder as you bring the *omoplata* to bear.

Leg entanglement – *Ashi garami*

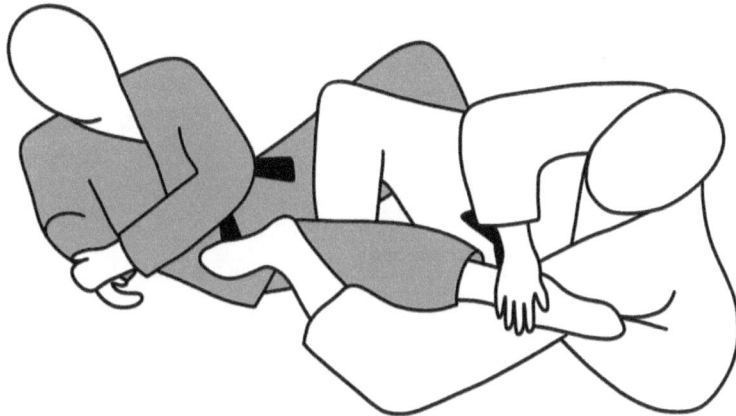

Basic technique: Tori sits back, facing uke, between uke's legs. Tori's left arm wraps over uke's lower right leg, trapping uke's ankle under tori's left armpit. Tori's left forearm sits under the lower calf, with the 'blade' of the inner forearm bone against uke's muscle. Tori's right hand grips uke's right lower leg on the shin. Tori's left hand locks onto tori's left forearm. Tori uses their left foot to lock over uke's right thigh, maintaining position. Tori's right leg is bent, and the shin is against the inside of uke's left leg, hopefully preventing kicks. The lock is completed as tori leans back onto uke's trapped foot and levers up with the left forearm, applying enough pressure to separate the ankle if necessary.

Effectiveness: Moderate. Tori lacks control of uke's upper body and torso, leaving uke with a lot of movement. The control of the non-trapped leg is also spotty, and the pain of the arm-blade under the leg isn't enough to overcome a determined person. Separating the ankle is useful, but requires a good deal of effort and a surprising range of movement.

Common problems:
- This is a sport grip, really. The right leg will help keep uke from kicking you in the face with their left foot, but you need to work at it.
- Interestingly, this lock is forbidden in judo, apparently. There's a fine line between applying sufficient pain to get a submission, and actually tearing apart the ankle joint.

Notes: If the pain is sufficient to really affect your opponent, you can use a variant of this lock to roll your opponent onto their belly to greatly increase your control.

Striking and kicking techniques – *Atemi waza*

Kicking Techniques	**103**
Front kick – *Mae geri*	104
Side kick – *Yoko geri*	105
Groin kick – *Kin geri*	106
Roundhouse kick – *Mawashi geri*	107
Back kick – *Ushiro geri*	108
Outer crescent kick – *Mikazuki geri*	109
Hook kick/Reverse roundhouse kick – *Ura mawashi geri*	110
Jumping front kick/Crane kick – *Mae tobi geri*	111
Hand Striking Techniques	**112**
Front punch – Footwork 1: *Oi tsuki*	114
Reverse punch – Footwork 2: *Gyaku tsuki*	115
Striking surfaces/Strike types	116
Forefist – *Seiken*	117
Knife hand – *Shuto*	117
Palm heel – *Shotei*	117
Spear hand – *Nuki te*	118
Ridge hand – *Haito*	118
Backfist – *Uraken*	118
Hammer fist – *Tetsui*	119
Sword peak hand – *Toho*	119
Elbow strikes – *Empi*	120

Historically, ju jutsu began on battlefields as a collection of combat methods for samurai who may have lost their primary weapons in the melee. The first known school of ju jutsu, the Takenouchi Ryu, was established in 1530, while Japan was still mired in internecine warfare and strife. These early systems of ju jutsu used very little in the way of striking techniques at all.

The probable reason for this lack of striking is very simple. If your opponent (on the battlefield) is wearing strong armour, it's extremely difficult to punch or kick hard enough to do real damage to them. Armour is meant to deflect attacks from weapons such as swords, spears and axes, and it's verifiably quite good at doing so. Deflecting a simple hand or foot strike is much simpler.

As a result, early ju jutsu was largely concerned with grappling, joint-locking and throwing. If you could come to grips with your armoured enemy, throw them to the ground and immobilise them with a joint-lock you could snatch out your *tanto* (dagger) and stab them through weak points the armour. Such striking as there was existed to surprise or destabilise the opponent, opening them up for grappling attacks.

Later, once Japan was unified by the Tokugawa Shogunate (the beginning of the Edo period, 1603 - 1868) battlefields became rare. Mass combat of any kind became far less common, and un-armoured duels became the most frequent form of samurai conflict. During this period, many more schools of ju-jutsu arose and techniques of striking were gradually incorporated into the art. Historically, this is also the period in which Japanese from Satsuma dominated Okinawa and forebade swords on that island. As a result, the native martial arts of Okinawa flourished, eventually spreading out as various forms of "kara te do" – 'empty hand way'. It is unlikely to be a coincidence, therefore, that the striking methods incorporated into ju jutsu during this time and later strongly resemble the basic strikes and kicks of karate.

There is also a historical counter-argument which suggests that ju jutsu was a well-developed martial art by this time, and in fact contributed to the development of karate rather than vice versa. Whichever version is historically correct, it is ultimately of far more interest that these strikes *were* incorporated into ju jutsu at some point. The change of ju jutsu from a system with almost no striking to a system that incorporated powerful and effective strikes at all ranges shows that the ju-jutsu masters of this time did not consider the art to be an unchanging, inviolate body of technique. Instead, it is clear they understood that for the art of ju jutsu to remain effective and relevant it had to be able to change, and to include methods that worked in the changing world.

This is an excellent example of the core principle of 'ju' – flexibility, yielding, or adaptability. It is also a clear lesson to any of us in modern times who might imagine that our ju jutsu is the final version, to be passed on without change from now to the end of the world. While the traditional *ko ryu* systems of ju jutsu are wholly worthy of respect and full of powerful, interesting techniques, they're still artifacts of another time and another culture. If ju jutsu is to remain effective and relevant as a defensive system, we have to be just as ready to make changes as were the masters of the Edo period three hundred and more years ago.

Kicking techniques

The muscles of the upper leg and buttocks are the largest and most powerful in the body. The legs are the longest limbs, offering the greatest reach. It follows that well-trained kicks are a valuable addition to your defensive arsenal. However since any kick must result in you taking at least one foot off the ground, kicking compromises your balance and your movement.

It's important to understand the crucial difference between a martial kick and an untrained 'football kick'. When untrained people kick, they tend to swing the leg from the hip pendulum fashion. The hip is pushed through, and the leg swings after it. Learn to recognize this action, because once you can identify it, avoiding an untrained kick is simple. The early transfer of weight to the off foot and the exaggerated hip movement of an untrained kicker will give you plenty of time to step offline and avoid the attack.

Trained martial kicks are delivered differently. A martial kick comes from a chambered knee, meaning that the knee of the kicking leg is deliberately lifted and pointed at the target, and then the leg unfolds explosively along the line of the kick. While a chambered knee is still something of a give-away, the chambering is actually part of the kicking process and can be done very quickly. Chambering the knee also allows for quicker balance recovery, and lines up the structure of your leg so as to deliver maximum damage.

Because the martial kick is not an instinctive movement, and because kicking compromises your balance, it's important to practice your kicking carefully, correctly, and extensively. Some useful tips:

- Break the kick into component movements. For most kicks, that's first: chambering the knee, then extending through the kick, then recovering to the chambered position, and finally replacing the foot to the start position on the floor. Practice these motions in order, but do them slowly and try to hold the proper position with each movement. This will help you ensure you maintain proper structure when you deliver the kick at speed.
- Always practice the recovery of the kick as extensively as the kick itself. Don't get used to hanging your foot out in the air at the end of a kick to check your form. The kick isn't complete until your foot is back on the ground contributing to your balance.
- Be acutely aware of your non-kicking foot. It's the one supplying balance and structure so that you can deliver power. The balance foot should be aligned along the direction that your kick is delivering power. If your balance foot is incorrectly placed or aligned, at best your kick will be weak. At worst, you'll wind up falling on your arse.
- Practicing high kicks is fine. It helps with your balance and flexibility. However in actual combat high kicks are also high-risk. The longer your foot is in the air, the longer your balance is compromised. And the higher your foot goes, the easier it is for your opponent to grab it and use it as a lever to overbalance you. Finally: I literally can't count the number of times I've seen enthusiastic practitioners show off an energetic high kick and wind up flat on their arses simply because the energy of the kick whisked their other foot out from under them as well. Practice high kicks, sure. But when you're using kicks for real, keep them low and fast.
- Be aware of your hands. Practice keeping your hands in a useful defensive position. It's true that throwing your hands in the opposite direction to your kick can give the kick a little more power, yes... but then if your kick misses, your opponent gets a golden opportunity to punch your lights out. Sacrifice the little extra power and keep your defensive guard intact.

Front kick – Mae geri

Basic action: Transfer weight to the off leg and chamber the kicking leg by lifting the knee. Ensure hips are square to target. With the knee aimed at the desired target shift your weight forward and extend your kicking leg explosively. Draw back with your toes to ensure the ball of the foot strikes the target. Snap foot back to chambered position then return to balanced stance.

Targets: This is a simple, powerful direct kick with potential to deliver a lot of force. Abdomen, kneecaps, groin and thighs are excellent targets. The kick may also be delivered high, to throat or face – but it becomes much more dangerous both for the opponent and yourself.

Variations: This kick can be delivered as a snapping, quick strike with an upwards lift (*mae geri keage*) – or you can push through with the hip more horizontally to drive into the opponent (*mae geri kekomi*). The second version obviously delivers more power, but as your weight is committed to the thrust of the kick you are off-balance and vulnerable if you miss. Note that with *mae geri keage* you return your foot to the starting position after the kick, whereas with *mae geri kekomi* you step through on the kicking foot to end the kick.

Common problems:
- Square your hips before delivering the kick. If your stance is angled or bladed so your hips face 45% away from your opponent, you can't deliver the kick with power. If you try to square your hips as you're chambering and delivering, the kick will be slow, and the motion will be easy to spot. Therefore, deliver the kick when you're square-on to your opponent for best effect.
- Even when you're practicing the thrust version of the kick, ensure you're training to 'stick the landing'. Do not allow the kick to overbalance you. If it's a snap kick, ensure you can return your foot to the starting point. If you're kicking all the way through, ensure you end in a clean, balanced stance with your hands in guard position.
- Make sure you keep your foot tense, toes pulled back. Striking with the toes is a good way to break or dislocate them. If you have trouble with that, try to imagine that you're delivering a stomp, driving forward with your heel. That will help you pull the top of your foot back for the kick.

Side kick – *Yoko geri*

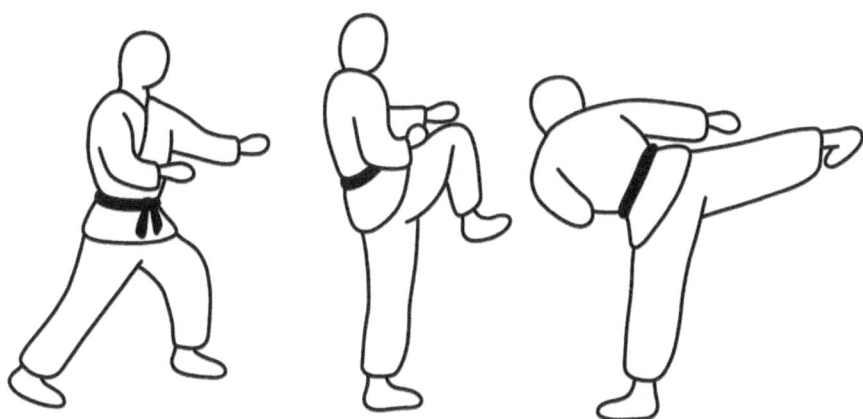

Basic action: From a front stance facing the opponent, transfer your weight to the off leg and chamber your kicking leg by lifting the knee towards your chest. To deliver the kick, thrust your foot explosively towards the target and pivot sharply on your off leg to push your hip through with the kick. As the kick strikes, your pivot action should have turned your support foot so that the heel points towards the target. Lean your upper body away: this counterbalances the weight of your leg, allows the leg to lift higher, and allows you to deliver the kick with a powerful 'stomping' action. Your kicking leg should be fully extended into the strike. Strike with the outer edge and heel of the foot, ensuring that your foot is either horizontal (parallel to the ground) or slightly turned so that your toes angle towards the ground. Recover to the chambered position, and pivot back into stance as you lower your kicking foot to the ground.

Targets: *Yoko geri* is one of the most powerful kicks, and the edge (or blade) of the foot is structurally strong. Kick into an opponents shin and rake downward to cause pain. Kick hard into the knee joint and stomp through to do serious damage to your opponent's ability to fight. Thigh muscles, groin, belly, liver and ribs are also excellent targets. You can also target throat and head – but there is danger of doing lethal damage, and of course there is greater risk to your own balance.

Variations: As with the front kick, there is a lifting, snapping version of *yoko geri*, but it is delivered without pivoting to drive through with the hip. It is also possible to sidestep into the kick with your off foot, greatly increasing the range of the kick.

Common problems:
- If you don't pivot properly and push through with the hip, it is difficult to generate power
- Keep the foot horizontal, or angled with the toes somewhat downward. If your toes turn to point upward your body structure is wrong. You won't generate power, and you may lose your balance.

Groin kick – *Kin geri*

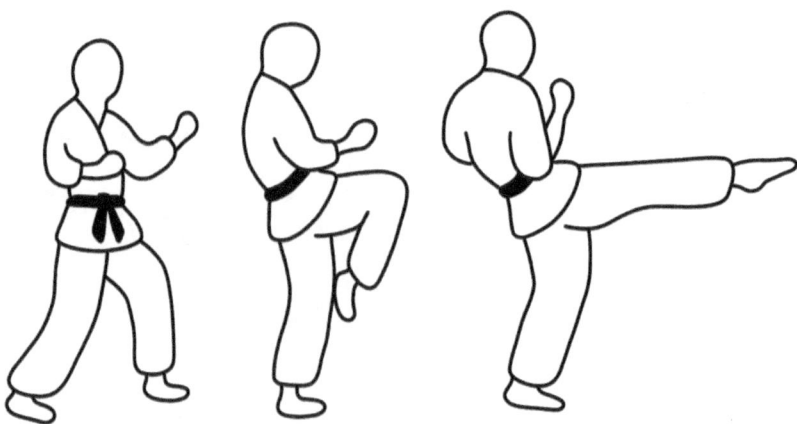

Basic action: From a front stance facing the opponent, shift balance to the off leg and chamber your kicking leg by lifting the right knee in front of you. Keep your foot pointed downward, toes extended. Kick forward and upward with a quick snapping action, driving your instep and ankle into the opponent's crotch. Recover through the chambered position, and return your foot to the ground in a balanced stance.

Targets: The term 'kin geri' comes from the Japanese 'kinteki' which rather amusingly translates as 'bullseye'. It's also a colloquial term for the male groin. So – yes. It's not like this kick is much good anywhere else, after all. It's really just a solid slap with the extended foot

Variations: You can deliver the kick a little deeper, striking with the lower part of your shin instead of the foot. This allows you to deliver a great deal more power as the shin is much more solid than the foot, and you won't be placing strain on the ankle joint.

One nice thing about *kin geri*, though, is that it can be delivered quickly off the front foot. If you've been pushed backwards, for example, you can fire off *kin geri* as you step back to stabilise yourself. Or you can keep your front foot light (place your weight in the back foot, as with a backward leaning stance or cat stance) and snap the kick quickly as your opponent attempts to approach.

Common problems:
- The real problem with kin geri is that it's just not as easy as most beginners think to kick a man squarely in the crotch. Every man knows that getting hit in the groin hurts like hell, so from an early age men begin to develop protective reflexes. Even a threatening movement towards the groin will often elicit an exaggerated defensive movement from the target. Kin geri is most useful when your opponent is already distracted in some fashion.
- Contrary to what many believe, kicking a female opponent in the crotch is very nearly as effective as kicking a male. Just like in men, the pubic region of women holds a lot of very sensitive tissue and organs. A strong kick to that area is extremely painful and debilitating.

Roundhouse kick – Mawashi geri

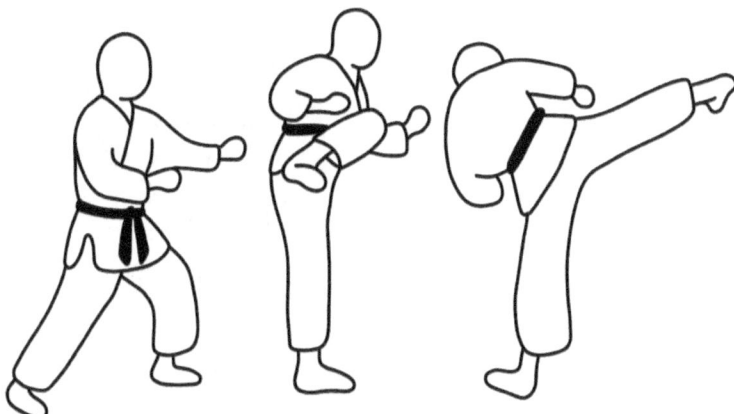

Basic action: Chamber the kicking leg by raising your knee to point along a line at least 45 degrees outside your target. Your lower leg should be inclined towards horizontal rather than held vertically. Pivot sharply across the line of the target and snap your leg explosively out and around while leaning your upper body back to maintain balance. Pull your toes back and strike with the ball of the foot. Recover through the chambering position and return your foot to a balanced posture.

Targets: Delivered properly, *mawashi geri* is an extremely powerful and destructive kick. Knees, thighs, abdomen and ribs are excellent targets if your opponent is front on to you. If the opponent is side on (bladed stance) the groin, liver, sternum and solar plexus are good options.

Variations:
- Instead of chambering the leg out to the side, you can chamber the kick in the forward direction with the lower leg vertical. This makes it look just like almost every other kick in your arsenal, which makes it a lot harder for your opponent to pick. It reduces the pivot and therefore the build-up and ultimately the power at delivery, but the classic side-chambered roundhouse is a pretty easy kick to see and avoid, so this variation has value.
- Instead of hauling your toe back to strike with the ball of the foot, you can attack from slightly closer to your opponent and strike with the instep and lower shin. This lacks the precision and penetration of the classic roundhouse kick – but let's be honest: it's a lot easier and safer. Keeping your toes pulled back at the angle required for the classic roundhouse kick is difficult, and if your toes make contact first, you're going to regret it.

Common problems:
- When pivoting, be sure to turn your grounded foot fully, so your toes point in the direction of the force of the kick.
- To get full power out of this kick, it's important to aim past the target with your knee. If you stop your pivot and deliver the kick with your knee pointed at the target, your knee will lock as your leg fully extends and you won't deliver full power to the target. You must aim your knee at least a handspan or so past your planned point of impact so your leg can strike with full force.

Back kick – *Ushiro geri*

Basic action: The target is directly behind, and your stance is forwards, not bladed. Chamber the kicking leg by raising the knee in front of you, lower leg vertical as usual. Looking behind you over the shoulder of your kicking leg, lean forward and drive the kick straight back with a powerful stomping action. You should strike your target with your heel, and your foot should be angled with the heel uppermost. Recover through the chambering position as usual, and return to a balanced posture.

Targets: *Ushiro geri* focuses power through the heel which allows for real penetration. Kicks to the knee are tricky, but the thigh muscles and groin are excellent targets. Solar plexus, liver and ribs work well too.

Variations:
- The turning or spinning back kick is common. To deliver this version of the kick, start by facing your opponent. Step across the centreline with your non-kicking foot, and turn that foot side-on to the opponent. Pick a target on the opponent. Now, quickly throw your shoulders and hips into a turn, placing your weight on the non-kicking foot and pivoting it so the heel faces the target. Meanwhile, lift your kicking foot to the chambered position. Turn your head and look for your target as you finish your turn – and complete the kick exactly as above.

Common problems:
- You must not deliver the kick without a clear line of sight to the target – whether you're turning, or simply delivering the basic version of the kick.
- Don't lean over too far. You will need to shift your balance to counter the weight of your kicking leg, but remember you need to sight your target over your shoulder.
- Remember the power comes from a thrust – a stomping action, not a turning and hooking action. Keep the heel high.

Outer crescent kick – *Mikazuki geri*

Basic action: From a forward leaning stance, the rear knee rises in a chambering action, but instead of rising straight forward the knee crosses the body. When the knee reaches the apex of the lift, the leg snaps sharply outward from the hip and the knee unfolds so the foot snaps outward and upward, with the outer edge of the foot hitting the target. The foot arcs around and down, returning to the grounded position.

Targets: Can be used against the head nicely. The arcing action of the kick lets you deliver it from closer range than most kicks, and it can be very unexpected. It can also be used against the opponent's hands and wrists, to clear their defensive guard.

Variations:
- You can reverse the action of *mikazuki geri*. When raising the knee to chamber, instead of going across the body you open the leg so the knee is outside the bodyline – not as far as with *mawashi geri*, but definitely not straight on. At the apex of the knee lift, the leg snaps across the body from the hip and the knee opens so the foot sweeps from outside to inside in an arc, striking the target with the sole of the foot. The arc finishes in the opposite direction, but the foot again returns to the original stance.
- A version of the crescent kick often seen in Tae Kwon Do systems sweeps the leg in a wide arc with little bending of the knee. It's almost a crescent axe kick, and doesn't do the same job as the version described here. It's difficult to generate much power in the horizontal plane with the 'wide arc' version, but it's easier to learn in the beginning.

Common problems:
- Power generation in *mikazuki geri* is difficult for some. The hips have to work hard to 'snap' the knee across, and you need to generate a kind of 'whipping' action with the unfolding of the knee.

Hook kick/Reverse roundhouse kick – *Ura mawashi geri*

Basic action: From a forward leaning stance, the back leg lifts to chamber the knee, but instead of lifting straight forward, the chambering action brings the knee across the line of the body. The foot still on the ground pivots sharply so the toe points away from the target, and the kick is completed by bending the knee and drawing with the hip to 'hook' the sole of the foot or the heel into the target.

Targets: Most often seen against the head, but this kick can be used as a clever low attack into the back of the opponent's knee, or into the calf muscle.

Variations:
- *Ura mawashi geri* is often delivered from a turn, which helps deliver more power to the kick. In this case, the rear foot steps across the line and pivot strongly away from uke. Tori whips the shoulders and upper body through the turn while chambering with the other knee. As soon as tori has a sight-line over their shoulder (or under their arm) on the target, the kicking leg opens, and the knee-bend 'hook' action occurs as the pivot finishes. It's a very pretty looking kick that shows up in lots of movies.

Common problems: Without the big turning action, *ura mawashi geri* lacks a certain amount of power. Speed and precision and good target choice make up for a lot, though. Don't exaggerate the pull-through of the hip in the hopes of increasing the power of the kick; you'll compromise your balance without gaining much.

Jumping front kick/Crane kick – Mae tobi geri

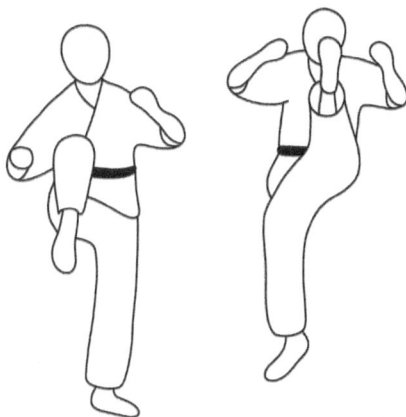

Basic technique: From a forward leaning stance, tori's back leg (right leg for purposes of description) rises and the knee chambers – but this chambering action serves not to kick, but to pull tori forward into a spring off the left foot. As tori lands onto the right foot from the leap, the left leg chambers and delivers a regular *mae geri* front kick.

Targets: All the same basic targets as any front-on kick

Variations: It is possible to spring, turn 360 degrees in the air and deliver this kick on landing. And doesn't it look lovely? Do feel free to practice it. It's very satisfying when you get it right. But if you imagine it will work the way it does in the movies, you're likely to be badly surprised. Reality has an unhappy way of thwarting beautiful spinning martial kicks...

Common problems: Some people have trouble acquiring the basic leap-and-kick rhythm. Try standing on one foot with the other knee raised. Next, hop onto the raised foot, and raise the opposite leg in its place. You're literally just hopping from foot to foot.

Next step is to hop, then kick. Still starting with one foot raised, you hop to that foot and raise the other directly into a kick. Once you've got that, start with both feet on the ground. Raise, hop, and kick – and you're doing *mae tobi geri*.

Notes:
- The original Karate Kid movie made this kick horribly famous. Please don't raise your arms like a demented windmill while standing on one leg and waiting for your opponent to react. Just... don't.
- In most situations, a simple *mae geri* is all it takes. But *mae tobi geri* can be very deceptive if you make the first knee-lift look like you're chambering to kick with that leg. There have been a few very nice knockouts in the MMA competitions delivered this way.
- In addition to being deceptive, the springing entry into this kick can gain a great deal of height or distance. If you need to make ground on an opponent, or if you really, really need to kick Godzilla under the chin, *mae tobi geri* is the kick for you.

Hand striking techniques

Not, you will notice, simply "punches". There are a lot of ways to hit the opposition. And while, of course, inside the MMA cages everyone balls their fists and goes hell-for-leather trying to club their adversary down, that doesn't mean there aren't other useful ways of striking with the hand area. It's worth noting that the 'Pancrase' MMA franchise did not allow closed-fist strikes, but a fighter named Bas Rutten (among others) became very well known for the power and efficacy of his open-hand work.

There are excellent reasons to have a good open-hand game. First, the small bones of the hand are vulnerable. Yes, if you throw a proper punch and clench your fist tightly at the point of impact you can give yourself some protection – but all that has to happen is for your opponent to move unexpectedly, and you'll hear a really depressing 'snap' noise as the metacarpals and phalanges (hand and finger bones) give way. There's a really good reason why pro fighters wear gloves, and it has nothing to do with protecting their opponents.

Secondly: the fist is a club, and that's all it can do. Open hands give you options: poking, grabbing, gouging, chopping – the hand is the most versatile of all tools. Turning it into a club and assuming that's the best it can do is simply stupid.

Thirdly: if you're fighting in self defense or defense of another, fists don't look good. Bystanders and onlookers will remember you as the person throwing punches. If your hands are open and you show your palms, it's a psychological sign that demonstrates peaceful intent. Bystanders will remember that your hands were open. Clearly, you weren't really trying to punch out the other guy's lights...

There are three critical elements to delivering a good strike: *speed, power* and *accuracy*.

Speed comes from relaxation. You deliver your strike with loose, relaxed muscles and tighten up at the end, as the strike impacts. Tensing up before impact will slow you down.

Accuracy comes from simple practice and repetition. Hit targets. Hit them a lot. Get a training partner with a nice, padded mitt and get them to move it around for you while you try to hit it. Do this a lot.

Power is a bit more problematic.

Size and strength are valuable in generating power. On the other hand, Bruce Lee was about the size of a Smurf and was notorious for being able to generate great power with his strikes – so you'd have to think technique would have something to do with it.

It does. There are three elements to generating power. One is appropriate footwork and body structure. With many strikes – mostly the linear ones – you can 'step in' and loan your bodyweight to the power of the strike. Jack Dempsey (a very successful boxer from the first half of the 20th century) was famous for striking with tremendous force, and he attributed much of that to what he called his 'drop-step', a method of bringing his bodyweight in behind his glove. By no great coincidence, Dempsey's 'drop-step' is pretty similar to a fencer's lunge, and to the advancing foot-step of a karate-style straight punch.

You can pick up the footwork for a basic lunge step pretty easily, but the second element of power generation takes more skill, more time to learn. The second element is a matter of recruiting all the right muscles to help put your attack on target – and to use none of the opposing muscles.

What does this mean? Consider the arm. The bicep is the big muscle on the inside, between the elbow and the shoulder. It folds your arm inward. On the opposite side of the humerus (that's the bone that runs from elbow to shoulder) is the triceps. This muscle structure pulls the arm open, helping you straighten it. Obviously, if you try to throw a punch while tightening your biceps, you're going to reduce your striking power because the biceps are trying to pull your fist back. So: when you're throwing a strike, you want to use the muscles that move the striking surface towards the opponent, and you want to keep the other muscles relaxed. That takes awareness, and practice.

The rest of your body plays a part too. You need a solid, well-grounded stance (with a few odd exceptions which don't fall under 'basics', so I won't be covering them) and you need to recruit the powerful muscles of your legs, and especially the abdomen – the 'core muscles.' This last is particularly obvious in what Japanese martial arts would call *'gyaku'* or reverse strikes. In these, instead of stepping in and striking with the hand over the lead foot to incorporate bodyweight, you strike with the hand on the opposite side to the lead foot — and a twist of the hips and torso lets you bring the most powerful muscles in your body to bear. This 'reverse' strike is the key to the boxer's devastating right hand power-punch.

The third method of incorporating power into a punch is odd: a kind of whip-snap action that accelerates your strike with a flowing, whipping action. These strikes aren't usually found in what we might call 'basic' ju jutsu, so we'll let them go for the time being. But if you're really interested in generating power with fast, whip-action strikes it's worth looking into some of the kung fu systems. And remember: ju jutsu is the art of what works. If you find something that works for you — borrow it, steal it, incorporate it, make it your own. There are hundreds of martial arts out there. All of them have something interesting to learn.

Two main kinds of strike

While there are many striking surfaces on the hand and arm, and many ways of delivering power in an attack, ultimately there's really only two types of strike in terms of direction. You can deliver a straight strike, in which the attacking hand travels in a straight line from you to the opponent, and there are arcing strikes, where the attack makes a curved line. Yes, you can start with one as a feint and shift to the other, but ultimately this is how it works biomechanically.

Straight strikes pretty much draw a straight line from your centre of mass and power to the point of contact. The more of your body structure you can get behind that straight line (as a rule of thumb) the more power you can generate. These straight shots are the ones that benefit from 'stepping in' to put your bodyweight into the power — for the long-reach shots, anyhow. If you use the reverse footwork, the power comes not from 'falling' into the long step, but from 'pushing off' with the back foot and turning the hips. Still a nice straight line between your centre of mass and power, and the point of impact.

Note that with a straight strike, you really want to keep your elbow tight and close to your bodyline. You're trying to create a straight line to deliver your bodyweight and muscle power. If you allow your arm to bend (letting the elbow come out from your body) you will drastically weaken your punching power. This is a critical element of basic punching technique: *keep your elbows in!*

Arcing strikes are more complex. At the simplest, you get the classic 'haymaker' of the untrained puncher. The right shoulder drops back, then swings forward and the right fist swoops around like a rock on a rope, accelerated by a body twist that will hopefully sling that fist into the side of your head. (It won't, though. Not unless you're very careless. The 'haymaker' is about the slowest, most telegraphed punch you'll ever encounter.) At the other extreme, a spinning backfist can seem to come out of nowhere if you don't know what to watch for, and the body turn allows for the generation of tremendous speed and power through the whiplash action. Note that arcing strikes include upward and downward curving strikes.

Most arcing strikes are delivered with the same basic footwork as the straight strikes, but they get less benefit from bodyweight simply because there's no nice, straight body-structural line between the impact and the direction of your body movement. As a result, arcing strikes depend more on the muscular power that you generate through the movements of the strikes themselves. That makes the twist of the torso and hips particularly important for close-in arcing strikes such as roundhouse elbows and boxing-style hooks.

Front punch – Footwork 1: *Oi tsuki*

Basic technique: Attacking hand is chambered to the hip, back of the hand downward. Leg on the same side as the attacking hand is back, in *zen kutsu dachi*. Opposite hand is extended or in a guard position. To deliver the strike, you step forward with an inward sweeping arc to land your foot in *zen kutsu dachi*. Hips snap through to square, and the lead arm snaps back to a chambered position to allow the shoulder frame to rotate around the body core and drive the striking arm forward as it extends through for the attack. The body should be relaxed during movement, but snap into tension at the moment of impact. The strike should hit at the same instant the lead foot comes down. The strike should immediately be withdrawn, unless you're taking a grip for a follow-up technique.

Notes:
- You don't really rise and fall with this forward step. The sweeping arc of the foot keeps your head level, but you do allow yourself to 'fall forward' into the strike to bring your bodyweight behind the technique. The front knee should be bent as the foot hits the ground, but you must not allow your knee to travel too far forward as you will overcommit your balance and be vulnerable – as well as placing great stress on the knee joint.
- Remember to exhale sharply – or deliver kiai – at the moment of impact, and inhale as you recover your position.
- You can cover quite a distance with this strike. Unfortunately, the opponent is quite likely to see it coming, especially if you chamber that hand on your hip. Starting from the hip and driving your fist in a straight forward line is good for learning which muscle groups you need to use... but not so good in actual self defense. You're better off with your hands up in a defensive posture.
- Keep your elbow tucked close to your body on all straight strikes. Remember, you want that straight line between your body-mass and the target. If your elbow hangs out and bends, the strike will be weak.

Reverse punch – *Footwork 2: Gyaku tsuki*

Basic technique: Attacking hand is chambered to the hip as before. Leg on the same side as the attacking hand is back, in *zen kutsu dachi*. Opposite hand is extended or in a guard position. To deliver the strike, rotate hips and torso sharply to face the target. Lead arm snaps back to a chambered position to allow the shoulder frame to rotate around the body core and drive the striking arm forward as it extends through for the attack. There should be a distinct 'pushing' feeling from the back foot through the hip, into the strike. The body should be relaxed during movement, but snap into tension at the moment of impact. The strike should immediately be withdrawn, unless you're taking a grip for a follow-up technique.

Notes:
- Obviously, this is a relatively short-range strike in comparison to *oi tsuki*. It is assumed that you have already stepped close with your lead leg, OR that your opponent has closed range and you have warded off a strike with your lead hand, allowing the reverse punch to come into play.
- Exhale sharply or deliver kiai with the strike. Inhale on recovery.
- Keep the elbow in tight while delivering straight strikes.
- Again: the hip chambering is good for teaching which muscle groups to recruit and use, but it's a terrible place to leave your hand during an actual fight. Keep your hands up where they can do some good in your defense.

Striking surfaces/Strike types

Using the footwork already shown, it's possible to deliver all the basic strikes commonly taught in ju jutsu. All you really need to consider is whether the strikes are straight or arcing, which surface makes contact, and what targets best suit each different strike.

Please note that as always, the strikes described and depicted here are really only the most basic variations and versions. This book exists as a reminder – a means of helping you remember names and basic elements. The actual strikes themselves can be as precise, as technical and as complex as your instructor wants them to be.

By way of example: my friend and colleague Bikram, who holds a 4th dan grading in Shotokan karate, speaks of an opportunity he had to train with a senior master in the art. Bikram says they spent more than two hours working on refining some of the most basic elements of a simple straight punch. He also says it's one of the best and most rewarding training sessions he's ever been part of.

My point is plain. Striking is just as complex and demanding as every other aspect of martial arts. It would be entirely possible to write a useful book for each and every striking technique individually, if one was prepared to discuss the myriad variations and situations involved. I have no intention of doing anything like that – so here you're getting a set of plain, simple, easy pointers which you can use to help remember the more basic striking techniques. If you really want them to work for you, you're going to have to pay attention to your instructor, practice with your fellow students as often as you can, and watch carefully to see how the techniques are applied by as many different people as possible.

Forefist – *Seiken*

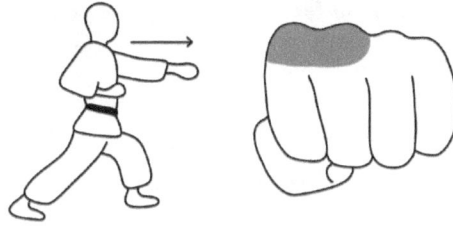

Striking surface: First two knuckles of closed fist.
Type: Strongest as a straight strike, but can be used for arcing 'hook' strikes with a strong turn of the body.
Targets: Look for soft body parts. Avoid strong bony areas such as the head. Liver, ribs, side of jaw, belly, groin, kidneys.
Problems: Fist must be held tightly, and the knuckles need to be properly aligned with the forearm or there's a risk of damage to the fingerbones (hard target) or the wrist (soft target.)

Knife hand – *Shuto*

Striking surface: Hand is open, held taut, fingers together, the whole slightly curved. Strike with the outer edge of the hand between the base of the little finger and the wrist.
Type: Arcing strike from a flexing elbow
Targets: Temples, jaw, neck, ears, throat, collarbone, ribs, axillary nerve in upper arm, radial nerve in lower arm.
Problems: Critical to strike with the palm edge. Misjudge your target and you will hit with the little finger. That won't go well.
Notes: Versatile. Cut in any direction you can swing your arm. May also be delivered palm down. And yes – this is the Legendary Karate Chop. Hiiiyah!

Palm heel – *Shotei*

Striking surface: Strong, padded bone structures at base of palm
Type: Strongest as a straight strike, but can arc, as in a hook attack.
Targets: The palm heel is a strong, resistant part of the body. You can attack the head safely with it – temples, nose, chin, side of jaw, hook behind the ear, ribs, groin.
Problems: Fingers must be tucked in safely and the hand must be cocked to strike with the correct surface. This is not a 'slap' but a powerful strike.
Notes: A good palm heel strike leaves you perfectly positioned to grab a handful of your opponent.

Spear hand – *Nuki te*

Striking surface: Rigidly held fingertips of stiffened, open hand.
Type: Straight strike.
Targets: Precision required. Fingers can be harmed by hard or resistant targets. Solar plexus, throat, groin, eyes, armpits.
Problems: Great accuracy and control are required. Even a small targeting error may wind up dislocating or breaking your fingers.
Notes: Low percentage. There are few situations where you wouldn't be better off with a different strike.

Ridge hand – *Haito*

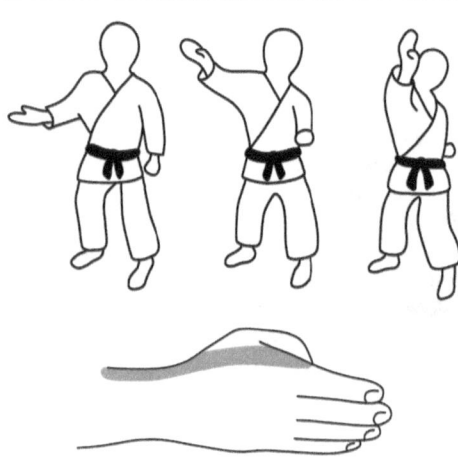

Striking surface: Thumb tucked into the hand, you strike with the radius bone of the forearm and the thumb-side edge of the hand. (The edge of hand is more technically correct, but the radius bone can hit harder without injury.)
Type: Arcing strike, delivered from whole-arm action starting at the shoulder.
Targets: Side and back of neck, collarbone, ribs (particularly floating ribs), liver, groin, ears, throat (if you're stepping past the opponent)
Problems: Keep the thumb tucked in safely, and be absolutely sure not to fully straighten your arm on impact. If your arm is fully straightened, you may place too much strain on your elbow and hyperextend it. This is a Very Bad Thing.
Notes: This is a much under-rated strike that can be delivered with great force at close range if you incorporate the forearm as a striking surface. (Technically *kote*, but delivered the same way) Consider stepping past your opponent and delivering a ridge-hand strike upwards into the crotch...

Backfist – *Uraken*

Striking surface: Back side of the first two knuckles of the closed fist.
Type: Arcing strike from elbow flexion.
Targets: Bridge of the nose, side of the jaw, ribs, ears.
Problems: Keep the fist aligned carefully and accurately to avoid damage to the smaller fingers.
Notes: If the hand remains relaxed and only fully forms a fist at the very last, it is possible to 'whip-strike' with *uraken* in a very quick, precise and painful fashion.

Hammer fist – *Tetsui*

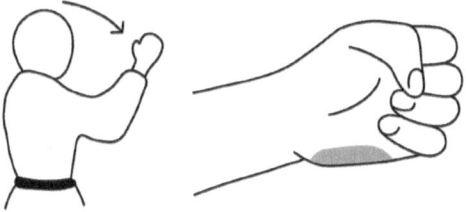

Striking surface: Muscular portion of closed fist at the base of the tightly curled little finger.
Type: Arcing strike from elbow and shoulder
Targets: The muscular padding of *tetsui* makes it ideal for hitting to the head. Temple, jaw, face, nose. It's also good for the collarbone, and can be used to strike an opponent's arms to 'clear a path' through their defense.
Problems: Fist must be kept very tight on impact. Don't mistakenly strike with the ulna!
Notes: Deliver horizontally as well as vertically. Use a whip action to increase horizontal power, and step in with your bodyweight to help bring power to vertical strikes.

Sword peak hand – *Toho*

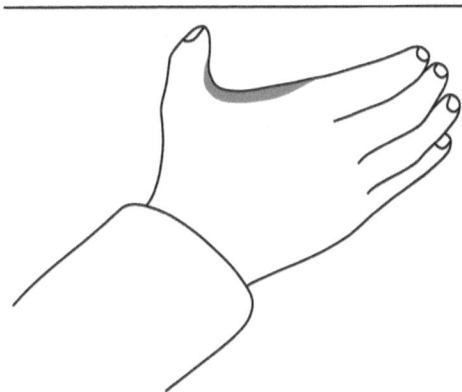

Striking surface: Inside of thumb, webbing, side of index finger, hand strongly tensed.
Type: Straight drive – horizontal or vertical. May also be used in an arc fashion, particularly to groin or throat.
Targets: The striking area outlined isn't as strongly reinforced as some other striking surfaces, but the curvature of *toho* makes it particularly good for a few specific targets. Driven strongly forward and upward into the armpits, *toho* attacks the nerve plexus in that area and sharply 'shocks' the victim. Applied as an attack to the throat, the natural curve of *toho* delivers a strike to the windpipe and the carotids all at once, and opens the way to grab the throat or drive through.
Problems: With the thumb open, care must be taken not to catch the thumb on anything as it can easily be dislocated by the force of your own strike.
Notes: Transitions easily into an 'eagle claw' grip at the throat or groin.

Elbow strikes – Empi

Striking surface: Flat, bony area on the outer forearm just in front of the elbow; flat, bony area on the outer upper arm just behind the elbow. The pointy bit of the elbow is NOT a useful striking surface. It is vulnerable, and prone to damage.

Type: Arcing strike (although you can drive straight with the elbow in certain positions)

Targets: Upper body and head. The elbow can deliver tremendous striking power, but works only at close range.

Problems: Close range only. You'll need to get through the opponent's defenses to deliver an elbow strike. Also, the point of the elbow is vulnerable. You need to take care to hit with the front or back of the elbow, not the tip.

Notes: The shoulder and upper arm are strong, but the main contribution to the force of an elbow strike comes from the body. Twisting the torso, driving with the legs and recruiting the abdominal muscles can make an elbow strike utterly devastating.

Blocking Techniques

Rising block – *Age uke*	123
Outside to inside block – *Soto uke*	124
Lower sweeping parry – *Gedan barai*	125
Cross block – *Juji uke*	126
Inside to outside block – *Uchi uke*	127
Scooping block – *Sukui uke*	128
Knife hand block – *Shuto uke*	129
Circling block – *Mawashi uke*	130

The term 'block' in English covers ways of using our own limbs to prevent an attack from striking more vulnerable targets on our body. It implies things like 'stopping', and 'blunting the force'. The mental picture we get of 'blocking' something is more or less putting an obstacle squarely in its path, stopping it cold.

The Japanese term used to describe these (partially, at least) defensive techniques is 'uke'. You should be familiar with that term by now. In Japanese martial arts, uke means 'to receive'.

Right away, that should change your mental picture. We're not blocking any more. We're *receiving*. And there are so very many ways to 'receive' a thing, right? In other words the concept of 'stopping the attack short' is just one possible variation of a much larger set of ideas and concepts.

At the core of 'receiving' is a simple goal: the destructive force of an opponent's attack should not reach the vulnerable target on your body at which it is aimed. But how many different ways might there be of achieving that simple goal? Here's a short list.

- Avoiding – no contact at all, just body movement
- Deflecting – an arm or leg is angled so that the incoming attack glances harmlessly off
- Redirecting – shift the force of the attack into a new line, harmless to you and possibly useful for creating a counterattack
- Intercepting – cut off an incoming attack before it builds sufficient force to be dangerous
- Trapping – capturing the attacking limb
- Pushing or pulling – using body movement and limbs to drive against the attack and off balance the opponent, or to trap the attack and draw the attacker to overbalance along the line of their force
- Absorbing – causing the incoming attack to dissipate against a limb by moving back with the attack.
- Damaging – a block that strikes into a vulnerable area of the attacker's limb, using the attacker's own force to deliver greater harm while also deflecting the attack.

Note that you can achieve more than one effect at a time. A two handed block that traps a low punch may also allow you to pull the opponent offbalance. An intercepting attack that hits the inside of the elbow of an arm drawn back to strike at you may also be extended to push the attacker backwards. These are simply examples. There are many possible combinations.

Of course, the shape and position of the most common blocks in ju jutsu are very similar to many karate blocks. While this probably reflects the influence of karate on ju jutsu, as noted earlier, it also reflects the simple fact that there are only so many ways the body can efficiently move. As always, you should learn the blocking techniques as taught by your own instructor in your own dojo. The list provided here is simply a reminder, a method of helping you visualize, understand, and remember the various blocks.

It is worth noting that in many systems, blocks are taught as strictly repeated motions with an 'end position' which more or less reflects the 'correctness' of the blocking movement. This method of teaching reflects a need to create patterned, reflexive movements that happen without the conscious thought of the student. As the student becomes more proficient with the individual techniques, the blocks are usually practiced in more complex situations against opponents providing committed, karate-style strikes. Again, this is a means of creating patterned, reflexive movements which are paired with a very particular system of attack.

And all of this can fall apart in self-defense if your attacker refuses to supply you with the right kind of incoming strikes.

It is important to practice your blocks against a wide variety of possible attacks. It's even more important to experiment with the blocks – see which movements are useful against what sort of attacks; discover different ways of utilising the same basic blocking movement against different attacks, or indeed, even against the same kind of attack. It is unquestionably vital for these blocks to be part of your muscle-memory, so you don't have to think about them. But if those crucial reflexes are linked inextricably to very particular sorts of attacks, the value and use of those reflexes in true self defense is questionable, to say the least.

The static method of demonstrating and learning blocks is all the more treacherous because it implies the blocking techniques are effective in the absence of body movement – evasion or entry. This idea needs to be stamped out completely. Your attacker launches a strike at the place they expect you to be. Right away, as a matter of principle you should simply *not be* where they want you to be. Move yourself. Use your feet!

There may be value to demonstrating the hand movements of a block in isolation, but those hand and arm movements should be connected to evasive or attacking body movements at the earliest opportunity. Standing still and receiving strikes in combat is foolish. It simply invites your opponent to keep striking until they get through. You need to move – to change the distance and the angle between you and your opponent, to give yourself the advantage and to take away your opponent's ability to strike you.

Finally: please remember that many of these blocking techniques are at their most effective against fully committed attacks. Don't expect to pull off clever hand-trapping blocks against someone who is skilled at boxing, for example, because they simply won't commit themselves into the attack in a way that will allow you to capture their hands.

Ju jutsu is not about two people fighting each other according to proper rules of any kind. ju jutsu began as a collection of efficient and brutal means of ending combat as quickly as possible. If you are unwillingly drawn into a 'boxing' or 'sparring' situation in self defense, you aren't using good ju jutsu and you need to change the situation to suit yourself. Mobility is key.

On the matter of mobility: ju jutsu is not karate. In common karate styles, these blocks are often used in a manner which largely maintains the distance between attacker and defender, and are generally intended to set up the defender to deliver a counter-strike.

In keeping with the principle of 'ju', ju jutsu is more flexible. It is possible to block, maintain distance and counterstrike, certainly. It is also possible to block and use body movement with the block to bypass or disrupt the opponent's guard, allowing a follow-up clinch, throw, joint-lock or strangling technique. Powerful 'hard-style' blocking isn't always the best choice, and it's important to understand the blocks thoroughly, and experiment with them to see what body movements work best for you.

Note: to make descriptions easier, the blocks may be described as using one hand or another. Relax. You can do them from either hand. Or both. Whatever. In fact, it's a good idea to practise them from either side.

Rising block – *Age uke*

Basic technique: Left hand is reaching up, and pulls down sharply as the right hand starts at the hip, forms a fist and rises up the centreline of your body, palm inwards. As the hand passes your face the forearm rotates with a snapping action to present the palm outwards and the elbow rises so that the hand stops a little higher than your head.

Blocking surface: Outer edge of the forearm

Purpose: *Age uke* is usually presented as a method of deflecting a straight strike to the face.

Variations: As depicted and performed in kata (the complex patterns of movement which are the primary teaching resource of classical karate) *age uke* is preceded with an upward 'reach' by the opposite hand. Then as the blocking hand rises, the 'reaching' hand pulls downward, by the hip.

This suggests that the interpretation of *age uke* as a deflecting, face-level block may not be the whole truth – that the 'blocking' action may be in the first hand that 'reaches', grabbing an attacker's arm which is then dragged downward, across tori's rising 'block' arm to attack the extended elbow of the opponent's arm.

Outside to inside block – *Soto uke*

Basic technique: Right hand begins at head height, forearm angled towards the top of the head, upper arm horizontal and extended to the side, palm facing forward, hand forming a fist. The forearm then sweeps down and across, stopping just past the centreline. Torso rotates to the left and the left arm is retracted to the hip. In the final position, the right fist is forward at just about chin level. The forearm is angled about 45 degrees from vertical, and the elbow is about one fist distance from the torso.

Blocking surface: Outer edge of the fore-arm

Purpose: *Soto uke* is supposed to deflect strikes aimed at the upper torso

Variations: While *soto uke* is taught with a closed fist, there is no reason the same motion cannot be performed with a knife hand to allow for a follow-up grab.

Lower sweeping parry – *Gedan barai*

Basic technique: Advancing onto the right leg, the right hand forms a fist and sweeps down from the left shoulder until the right arm is directly over the right thigh. At the same time the left hand snaps back to chamber at the hip. The back is kept straight, and weight rests on the front leg.

Blocking surface: Outer edge of forearm and fist

Purpose: This action is meant to sweep aside an attack to the lower body or upper leg. The body faces forward, hips angled no more than 45 degrees.

Variations:
- Can be done in retreat – left leg steps back and right arm sweeps down into position over right leg.
- A softer, more mobile version of this block can be done from a dodging action. Instead of stepping forward into a deep stance and sweeping powerfully with a closed fist, you can turn your hips and step lightly forward (into something like a cat stance, with the front foot farther forward than usual) to move your hips and body off the line of the strike. The arm sweeps down as usual, but the hand can remain open to catch or scoop. This version of *gedan barai* keeps your bodyweight relatively high, and allows you to move forward quickly to bypass your opponent's guard.

Cross block – Juji uke

Basic technique: Hands come together driving outward from the body and crossing at the wrists to meet an incoming attack.

Blocking surface: Outer edge of both wrists simultaneously

Purpose: Juji uke is intended to stop and potentially capture an attacking limb

Variations: Can be done high or low, with open hands or closed fists. Juji uke is often taught as a 'stopping' block that completely absorbs the power of an incoming attack, but it can also be used to redirect an attacking limb into position for a capture or jointlock technique.

Notes: It is crucial to remember to use protective body movements with this block, as with all blocks. While juji uke permits the strength of both arms to be incorporated into the blocking action, that may not be sufficient to absorb the power of a strong kick, or to stop the attack of a large, powerful person. Remember your attacker intends that the power of their attack should be greatest at their chosen target point – so move off that point and use juji uke to intercept the attack early before full power has developed, or catch it late when the attacker is overextended.

Inside to outside block — *Uchi uke*

Basic technique: Blocking hand starts on the opposite hip, forearm across the body, hand formed into a fist. The hand snaps up and across until the forearm is aligned to the outside edge of the torso. The fist should end just about at shoulder height, back of the hand facing forward, with the forearm about 45 degrees off vertical. The opposite arm snaps back at the same time to chamber at the hip, causing the torso to turn towards the blocking arm.

Blocking surface: Inner edge of the fore-arm

Purpose: *Uchi uke* is intended to deflect an incoming strike to the upper body by pushing it outside the bodyline.

Variations: The snapping action allows this block to be used as a strike to a vulnerable part of the attacker's arm. If *uchi uke* is used more softly, with greater body movement and footwork it can allow for entry to grappling using the blocking arm as a lead.

Scooping block – *Sukui uke*

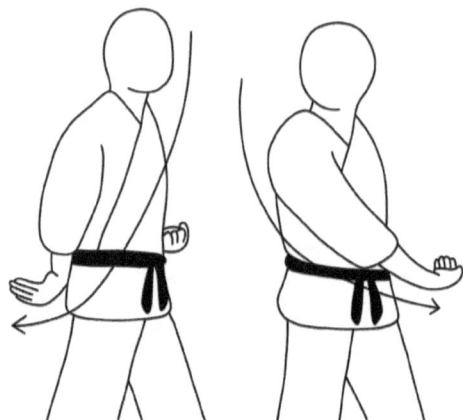

Basic technique: Can be done to either side. Hand starts high, above the opposite shoulder to the direction of the scooping movement. As the arm swings down across the body, the torso turns to follow, helping the arm cross the centreline. At the bottom of the arc, the open hand curls upward, palm facing the direction of the scooping action.

Blocking surface: Palm, wrist, inner forearm.

Purpose: *Sukui uke* is generally taught for the purpose of 'scooping' and catching an incoming kick attack.

Variations: Using your feet to move with the scoop rather than simply turning the torso allows you to close with your attacker if desired, or to set yourself so that you can drag the leg forward and overextend the attacker.

Knife hand block – *Shuto uke*

Basic technique: Left hand begins above the right shoulder, palm down, fingers extended. Advancing onto the left foot, the left hand sweeps down across the body ending with the left hand at shoulder height, palm outward, arm and hand in line with the outer edge of the torso. The hand is tightened and set in the 'knife hand' configuration, wrist slightly cocked.

Blocking surface: Outer edge of the palm

Purpose: *Shuto uke* is usually taught as an attacking block, designed to strike at vulnerable areas of an attacker's arm. It can protect from the lower torso up to the head.

Variations: If *shuto uke* is performed with a relaxed wrist, you can block with the outer edge of the fore-arm just below the wrist joint, and the impact will let you flick your relaxed, open hand over the upper surface of the incoming arm, potentially trapping it. This is a softer blocking technique which still provides safety, but permits rapid transition to limb control, joint locking or grappling if the gripping action is successful.

This variation is particularly useful if done – as is common with *shuto uke* – from *kokutsu dachi*, as the stance allows you to 'sink back' and absorb some of the power of the incoming strike with your body motion before springing forward in attack.

Circling block – Mawashi uke

Basic technique: Left hand, palm facing to the right, sweeps up and pushes across to the right at face level to deflect an incoming strike. In classical karate this is followed quickly by the right hand sweeping up, palm facing left, and pushing across to the right with the back of the hand. The idea is to deflect the incoming strike and instantly move it farther offline by 'feeding' from the palm of the left hand to the back of the right hand.

Blocking surface: Palm of blocking hand

Purpose: Protect from head-level strike and open the opponent's guard.

Variations: The deflecting push of the palm doesn't have to feed to the opposite hand. You can use this block to deflect and incoming straight strike and quickly move in along the outside of the opponent's arm. This is an excellent entry for a number of throws and strangles. If your opponent is slow to withdraw the arm after the strike, this is also an excellent opportunity to attack the straight elbow by bringing up your other hand on the palm-side of their arm to trap the elbow between your opposed hands.

Notes: Wax on, wax off... Oh, and for pity's sake move your feet. Get your face and body out of the line of the attack.

Strangling and choking techniques – *Shime waza*

Rear naked choke – *Hadaka jime*	132
Triangle choke – *Sankaku jime*	133
Sliding collar choke – *Okuri eri jime*	134
Single wing choke – *Kata ha jime*	135
Cross chokes – *Juji jime*	136
Hell choke – *Jigoku jime*	137
Front naked choke/Guillotine choke – *Mae hadaka jime*	138
Sleeve wheel choke – *Sode guruma jime*	139
Two-handed choke/Baseball-bat choke – *Morote jime*	140

Strangling and choking techniques are among the most dangerous attacks available. The terms are more or less interchangeable, but there are two physical methods of attack at work which need to be explained.

Most people think of 'choking' as the result of compression of the trachea – the windpipe – preventing air from reaching the lungs. This certainly can happen, and if the choke is left in place long enough, lack of air will lead to lack of oxygen in the blood, which will result in brain death after a few minutes.

Choking the airway, however, is extremely painful. It is also quite alarming to the victim, and they will struggle violently to escape. On top of that, cutting off the airway still leaves the reserve of air in the lungs, so it takes anywhere up to three minutes to knock someone out this way. Three minutes of restraining a person who is struggling for their life is a challenge no matter how good you are. There is a more efficient way.

The carotid arteries run up either side of the neck, beside the trachea and forward of the big neck muscles. These arteries supply almost all the blood to the brain. Direct compression of the carotid arteries will black out a victim very quickly indeed: usually less than ten seconds of full compression is adequate. It is also far less painful than direct pressure to the trachea, so by the time the victim realizes anything is seriously wrong, they have only a few seconds of consciousness left.

It follows that properly applied carotid strangles are extremely effective – and also extremely dangerous. Strangles of any kind should only ever be practised under observation and supervision, preferably by someone who has at the very least basic first aid certification. Applying a carotid strangle for ten to twenty seconds leads to unconsciousness. Leaving the strangle in place for two or three minutes deprives the brain of oxygen, possibly leading to irreparable damage. Keeping the strangle in place for very little longer will cause complete brain death.

STRANGLING TECHNIQUES KILL PEOPLE.
Do not practice strangling techniques except under carefully controlled circumstances. **Do not** use them in self defense or defense of another unless there is no other safe way to handle the situation. **Do not** leave a strangle in place longer than is necessary to overcome your opponent. Once the opponent is unconscious, if possible you should place them in the recovery position and ensure that their pulse and respiration are unimpaired. Should you accidentally black out a training partner, place them in the recovery position and alert your instructor immediately.

Rear naked choke – *Hadaka jime*

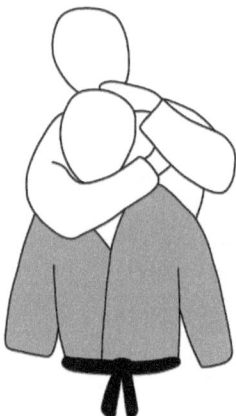

Basic technique: (Right handed version) Tori's right arm passes over uke's right shoulder from behind. Tori slips their right elbow directly under uke's chin and pulls their arm in tightly against uke's neck. Keeping their forearm in contact with uke's chest and collarbone, tori bends their right arm so that their right thumb passes up behind uke's ear and the blade of their forearm presses tightly against uke's neck, opposing the pressure of tori's right biceps on the opposite side of the neck. Tori passes their left arm over uke's left shoulder, with the arm bent, and locks their right hand onto their left biceps. Tori's places their left palm against the back of uke's head on the right hand side. Tori pulls uke backwards to offbalance them, so that uke is forced to lean into tori to remain upright. Tori scissors their right arm tightly closed, locking the strangle in place with the left hand and arm grip.

Variations: *Hadaka jime* is a versatile strangle that does not require a sleeve or jacket grip. It can be done standing, kneeling, sitting, or even lying down so long as you are behind the opponent.

Common problems:
- Get the elbow directly under the chin. That way your arm scissors the carotids properly. If you're off-centre you'll wind up putting pressure on the trachea and less pressure on the carotids.
- Do NOT forget to haul your opponent back and break their balance, if this is applied in a stand-up situation.
- DON'T hang your left arm out straight over the opponent's shoulder to 'lock on' to the bicep with the right hand. Put your left arm in position already bent – or your opponent can grab it and potentially even dislocate your elbow.

Notes: This strangle is extremely dangerous. It is also now widely known, courtesy of the popularity of mixed martial arts on television. It is imperative you learn and practice escapes from common versions of this choke – particularly from the standing position. Escape measures must be applied at the earliest instant. Once this strangle is locked in, you've got scant few seconds of consciousness left.

Triangle choke – *Sankaku jime*

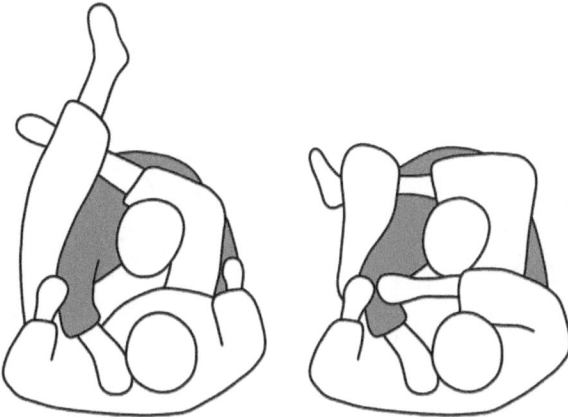

Basic technique: From the closed guard position, tori throws their right leg over uke's left shoulder when uke withdraws their left hand prior to an escape attempt. Tori maintains control with two hands over uke's right hand, and quickly puts their left leg over their right foot. Tori pulls their right foot down towards their body to tighten the strangle, and try to 'lock' it in place by tucking the right foot into the back of their left knee. Tori pulls uke's right arm towards themself to make it easier to turn uke's body and tighten the strangle. To finish the strangle, tori closes the angle of their right knee powerfully, while drawing uke's right arm towards themself. Tori's right leg will shut down uke's left carotid, and possibly more.

Variations: There is an excellent variation on this strangle which is done from behind. The right leg goes over uke's right shoulder and across the front of the body. Uke's left arm is pulled up towards tori, and as tori locks their right foot into place with their left knee, tori can also draw the left arm up and back into a very effective straight armlock. The combination of the straight armlock with the strangle is devastating.

Common problems:
- Always remember to pull the arm on the other side to your strangling leg!
- You may find it difficult to bend your right leg far enough to trap it behind your left knee. Maintain control over uke's right arm with your right arm, and use your left hand to pull your right foot down to assist the strangle.

Notes: Obviously, *sankaku jime* is a ground-fighting strangle. And of course, in classical, defensive ju jutsu you don't want to be spending too much time on the ground if you can avoid it. Nevertheless, this is a useful and very powerful technique. It engages some of the strongest muscles in your body, making it difficult for your opponent to break free. Further, it can be done without a jacket on either you or your opponent.

If you do use it, be wary of a powerful opponent standing up inside your grip, and lifting you for the slam. You'll probably want to change tactics quickly if you find yourself in that position – unless you're confident that the strangle is close to completion.

Sliding collar choke – *Okuri eri jime*

Basic technique: Tori is behind uke. Tori's head sits against the left side of uke's head. Tori's right hand reaches around, across uke's throat beneath the jawline and grabs uke's collar as far back behind uke's left ear as tori can reach. Tori's left hand slips under uke's left arm and reaches across to grasp uke's right lapel just below tori's right forearm. To apply the strangle, tori pulls down and across with the left hand, while pulling across and back with the right hand – the two pulling actions opposing one another. If tori's collar grip is deep enough, uke's left carotid will be shut down and painful pressure will be applied to uke's trachea. To finish the strangle and control uke safely, tori locks down uke's right arm with their right leg, and locks their feet in front of uke's hips.

Variations: This can be carried out from the front in similar fashion, although it's harder to control uke from that position. In a pinch, you can do this to someone wearing a tie and a collar if the tie is a decently strong one. (This would be one reason why I personally avoid wearing ties...)

Common problems:
- Take the collar grip as deeply as possible. Get your hand right back behind their ear, whether you're doing it from in front or from behind.
- Remember you must reach all the way across to the opposite lapel.

Notes: Not a great defensive strangle. Highly dependent on uke's clothing – although if you happen to have a convenient scarf, belt or rope you can loop it around uke's throat and make a very effective choking weapon with this configuration.

Single wing choke – *Kata ha jime*

Basic technique: From behind, tori slides their left arm under uke's left arm, raising uke's left arm so that tori's arm can pass behind uke's head. Tori's right arm passes under uke's chin, reaching back to grab uke's collar as far back behind uke's left ear as possible. Tori may lock their left hand on their right forearm, or simply pressure the back of uke's head. The strangle is applied by pulling strongly with the right hand on uke's collar, cutting off the left carotid and potentially scissoring the right carotid with tori's right fore-arm.

Variations: While this is usually taught from a kneeling position, this strangle may be 'locked in' by tori wrapping their legs around uke's waist to control from the back.

Common problems:
- Reach deep for the collar grip. No, deeper than that.
- The raised left arm doesn't really contribute to the strangle other than keeping uke in a convenient sort of position. It does, however, stop uke using the arm to break the strangle or attack you.

Notes: Primarily a sporting technique. Can be used as a surprise take-away to overpower someone from behind – but the rear naked choke is easier and more reliable for this purpose.

Cross chokes – *Juji jime*

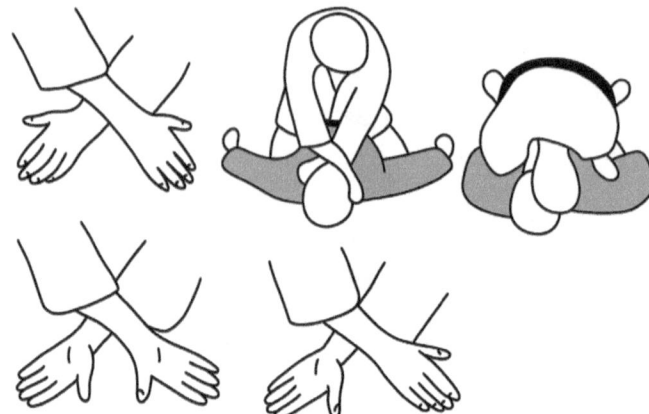

Basic technique: All three of these chokes use the same basic mechanics. Tori extends both arms crossed at the wrist or forearm, and reaches as deeply as possible behind uke's head to grasp uke's collar on either side. Tori then holds tightly to the collar and scissors the wrists across uke's throat, pulling uke closely into the strangle and cutting off the carotids. *Nami juji jime* translates as normal cross choke, and biomechanically works best from the top mount. For this choke, tori's thumbs are tucked under uke's collar (palms down) for grip. *Gyaku juji jime* (reverse cross choke) calls for the fingers to be tucked under the collar (palms upward), and works better when tori is on the bottom, pulling uke down. *Kata juji jime* (half cross choke) has one palm up and one down.

Variations: Can be done from top mount, or from bottom guard. Or any position where tori faces uke, really. Except where heads are at opposite ends, obviously...

Common problems:
- Remembering the individual names of these three chokes is annoying. They all work basically the same way, with relatively minor biomechanical differences.
- Get really deep on that collar. Seriously. Why do I have to keep telling you this?

Notes: All these chokes require a good, strong collar on uke. On top of that, they're all done from the front, which leaves you vulnerable to counter-attack by strikes. They're fine for sport, but if you use them defensively you'll want to offbalance and overpower your opponent so you can exert real control over their options until they pass out from the choke.

Hell choke – *Jigoku jime*

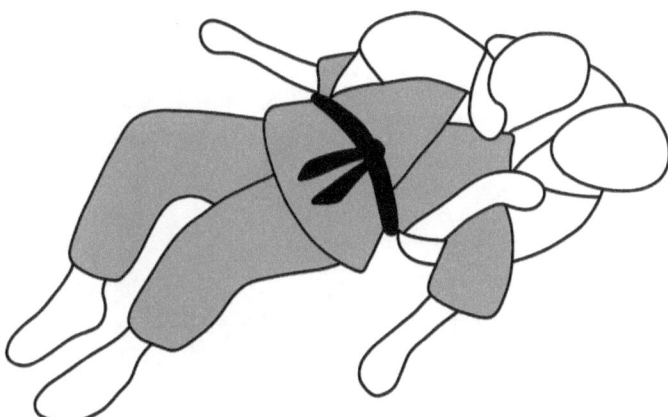

Basic technique: Tori's right hand reaches over uke's right shoulder from behind, around the throat to grasp uke's left collar as far back behind the ear as possible. Tori's right leg goes over uke's right arm to restrain it. Tori's left arm comes up from under uke's left arm and grabs onto tori's collar to lock down uke's left arm. The strangle is applied by pulling across and back with the right hand, cutting off uke's left carotid.

Variations: This one kind of slides into versions of *kata ha jime*.

Common problems:
- You know what I'm going to tell you, right? Go deep on the collar!

Notes: Why is this called 'hell choke'? I don't know, but I have a theory. One of the common entries for this choke happens when uke panics during groundfighting and decides to 'turtle up' as a defense – hunkering down on hands and knees and covering up their head.

This is not a wise choice. If you did it on the street, you'd be inviting your opponent to stand up and kick your ribs into splinters. But even in civilised judo-style groundplay where striking isn't permitted, it's still not great because tori can work that hand under for the collar grip, then roll right over you to flip you with their body weight – and the next thing you know you're on your back with tori wrapped around you like a starfish on a particularly tasty-looking scallop, choking your lights out with *jigoku jime*. You get about six seconds to wonder what the hell happened and what kind of hell you've blundered into, and then it's lights out.

Front naked choke/Guillotine choke – *Mae hadaka jime*

Basic technique: From a closed guard position, tori throws their right arm over uke's neck, passing their forearm under uke's throat and bringing the head down beside tori's torso. Tori's left hand reaches in under uke to link with the right hand. With the blade of tori's right fore-arm against uke's throat, tori tightens the leg-grip, then leans back strongly as if trying to pull uke's head off. As tori leans back, they also use their leg grip to push uke in the opposite direction, increasing strength of the pull. This is not a blood choke that affects the carotids. It comes on to the trachea, causing intense pain and frequently a lot of fear. It also takes more time than the blood chokes to work, so tori may need to maintain the position for a couple of minutes.

Variations: This choke is often performed from a standing position after uke has attempted a tackle or takedown. It isn't particularly effective as a standing control as there are a number of ways to break loose, and the sheer pain of the technique is likely to spook your opponent into struggling with all the violence they can muster – so the standing version often transitions into the better-controlled ground version.

Common problems: Because this is an airway compression more than a blood choke, it takes time to subdue the opponent. Determined opponents can and will struggle with great strength and it can be difficult to join the hands and maintain head control long enough to make it work.

Notes: The sheer pain of having your windpipe compressed by a solidly placed forearm is pretty upsetting. Trained persons in a dojo will tap when they've had enough. People without training won't instinctively tap – and may very well do seriously crazy stuff because they think you're trying to kill them. Good, solid sports technique – but not so good for defense except as a transition to another means of control.

Sleeve wheel choke – *Sode guruma jime*

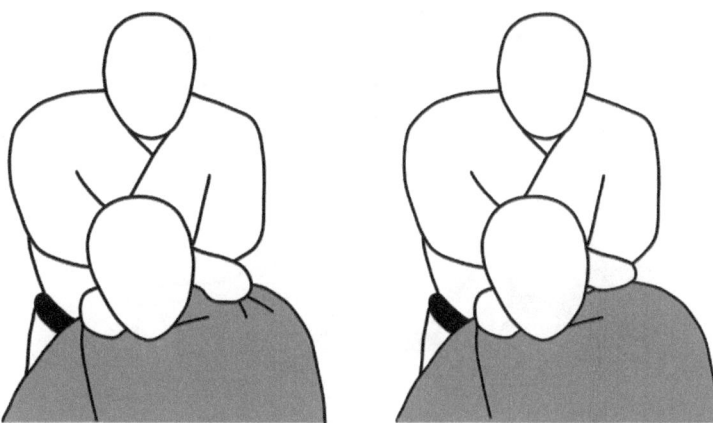

Basic technique: From behind, tori reaches their left arm over uke's left shoulder and grabs the left lapel of uke's gi. Tori yanks up and pushes that gi across uke's throat so the collar winds tightly around the left side of uke's neck. Tori's right hand clamps onto tori's left forearm, allowing tori's right forearm to apply pressure to the back of uke's neck. The strangle is brought on by pushing hard with the left hand to drag the collar against the throat, and scissoring down with the right forearm to push uke's head and neck into the collar.

Variations: There's a tonne. The version depicted here is nice and simple, but it exists largely because of judo rules regarding what can be used to apply pressure to the neck, and what can't. Astute observers will realise that the sleeve and the gi aren't actually needed; tori can apply a nasty choke just by scissoring the two forearms from this position. (Of course, uke can simply lunge forward to escape – the gi grip is handy, yeah.)

You can do this strangle in groundfighting from above or below by putting one forearm in front of uke's neck, and one behind, hands pointing opposite directions. Each hand grabs the sleeve of the other arm, catching uke's throat in a fore-arm scissors. The pain of the windpipe crush will usually drive uke to turn their head – which brings the choke directly onto the carotids, and game over.

There's an extremely nice no-sleeve standing version as well. Tori slips outside a right-hand front punch from uke. Tori's right arm comes up underneath uke's extended right arm, and cuts down into uke's left-side neck and collarbone with *haito uchi*, the ridge hand strike. This offbalances uke, forcing their head down and towards tori's left. Tori now reaches over uke's right arm with their left, seizing their own right forearm or wrist as close to uke's throat as possible. The left forearm now scissors against the right hand, trapping uke's throat. Tori overbears uke, dragging them close in the choke and hanging them in place until they pass out or submit.

Common problems:
- However it's done, there must be a close, tight scissoring action on uke's throat.

Notes: Versatile, and effective even without a jacket – but care must be taken to lock it in place and prevent escape.

Two-handed choke/Baseball-bat choke – Morote jime

Basic technique: Tori clasps hands palm to palm. Left forearm sits over uke's right shoulder, right forearm tucks into the left side of uke's neck. To apply the choke, tori twists their torso to push the right elbow across uke's body, causing the forearms to scissor into uke's neck.

Variations: Works even better if tori takes a grip on uke's gi instead, while still keeping the arms in the same orientation.

Common problems:
- If uke has a thick neck, you'll have to figure out how to adjust your handgrip.
- Done from the standing position, tori is vulnerable to all kinds of counter-attacks from uke

Notes:
- From the standing position, tori can turn across with their right hip and use the baseball bat choke as the grip for a really nasty hip throw
- This choke can be done on the ground. There are ground-based variations which are much safer for tori because tori can limit uke's movement to reduce possible counter attacks.
- Tori can apply this choke with or without the gi from standing position, and then simply drop onto their left side, hanging from uke's neck and dragging uke down to the ground as well. This is a brute of a technique in sport-fighting, and will do the same job in defense – but of course, going to the ground is a last resort in self defense.

Hold-down techniques – *Osaekomi waza*

Scarf hold – *Kesa gatame*	142
Shoulder hold – *Kata gatame*	143
Chest hold – *Mune gatame*	144
Side four-quarters hold – *Yoko shiho gatame*	145
Upper four quarters hold – *Kami shiho gatame*	146
Upper four quarters hold – *Tate shiho gatame*	147
Reverse scarf hold – *Ushiro kesa gatame*	148
Closed guard – *Do osae*	149
Rear mount	150

Most of the common hold-down techniques taught in ju jutsu are similar to those in judo, which makes them questionable for defense. Judo is a sporting system, and the hold-downs generally pin uke on their back which is inefficient as it leaves uke with a great deal of limb mobility. If you really want to immobilise someone, look at police around the world: they put suspects face-down on the ground because it's harder for someone who is face down to see, to move, and to resist.

With the rise in popularity of Brazilian jiu jitsu, a few more hold-downs have entered common use – but again, the sporting nature of BJJ often reduces the defensive qualities of the hold down techniques. For purposes of this book, I have differentiated between 'true' *osaekomi waza*, or techniques where both people are on the ground, versus more hostile techniques where one person is more or less upright, controlling the grounded person with a painful and dangerous joint lock or similar.

Even if the classic groundfighting holds of judo aren't the best from a self-defense standpoint, they still serve an important purpose. Learning to apply these holds, and to move easily between them while controlling a resisting opponent will help develop important skills of mobility and ground tactics. Even though it may not be desirable to fight on the ground, you must remember: you do not always control the way a conflict unfolds. You may find yourself surprised on the ground, or you may simply wind up on the ground by accident. If you don't know how to move and fight on the ground, you're at a serious disadvantage to anyone who does.

The key concepts to take away here are *mobility, adaptability, close contact* and *use of body weight*. Most of these hold-downs are used in a sporting context to control a non-striking opponent, and to wear them down by making it hard to breathe and forcing the opponent to burn energy in struggling to escape. A tired, out-of-breath opponent is likely to take risks and make mistakes, opening the way for a submission attack such as a strangle or a joint-lock. These same tactics work against an opponent who is willing to strike, gouge, or bite. You simply have to be more wary, exert better control over their limbs and weapons – and be prepared to use strikes yourself.

It is worth noting that many of the positions taught from a judo perspective are now widely known from Brazilian jiu jitsu in a different fashion. BJJ stresses the utility and purpose of the holds rather than precise replication of the positions. For example, *yoko shiho gatame* (judo) becomes 'side control' in BJJ. And rather than being focused on exactly where arms and hands and legs go, BJJ pays attention to critical elements: where uke's weight should be in relation to tori, and how tori should position themself to control uke's movements in different directions. This approach offers a better means of understanding how the different holds work in actual defense.

Above all, I can't stress enough that what makes any of these hold-down techniques work is continual practice against resisting opponents. It's not enough to 'master' individual holds. You have to be able to move between holds, change position to maintain control, use your own body weight as a weapon during the struggle, and avoid giving opportunities to your opponent. The only way to make these hold-downs relevant and useful is hard, repeated practice. You need training space, and you need training partners. There's no alternative.

Scarf hold – Kesa gatame

Description: Uke is on the floor, on their back. Tori sits with their right hip snugly against uke's ribs, legs splayed for stability. Tori control's uke's head and neck with their right arm, and controls uke's right arm with their left, gripping firmly against the elbow. Tori places their weight on uke's upper body and wraps uke's head and neck tightly into tori's chest. Tori should keep their head forward and down to help prevent escape.

Common problems: If tori lifts their head or leans back across uke's body at all, uke may be able to overbalance them and escape. Failing to properly control uke's right elbow may allow uke to slip the arm and counter-attack. Not splaying the legs correctly will create a weak point in tori's balance and uke may be able to roll them off.

Defensive uses: Easily entered after a throw. Allows good control of untrained opponents, and combined with a neck crank can make uke's breathing difficult, establishing a submission. However, this hold keeps tori on the ground as well limiting mobility and observation. Best used in sporting context.

Basic escapes: Uke may try to wrap both legs around tori's back leg to entrap it, allowing uke to twist out from under tori's right arm grip. Uke may bridge their hips up in an attempt to overthrow tori, and follow that quickly with a leftward roll pulling strongly with the right arm in an effort to throw tori across their body. Freeing the right arm will allow uke to counterattack, but care should be taken from this inferior position as tori has better attacking options.

Basic changes and variations: If uke frees their right arm, tori can catch the wrist and establish *kesa garami*. If uke bends the arm up, tori can trap the elbow with the side of their head and push into *kata gatame*.

Shoulder hold – *Kata gatame*

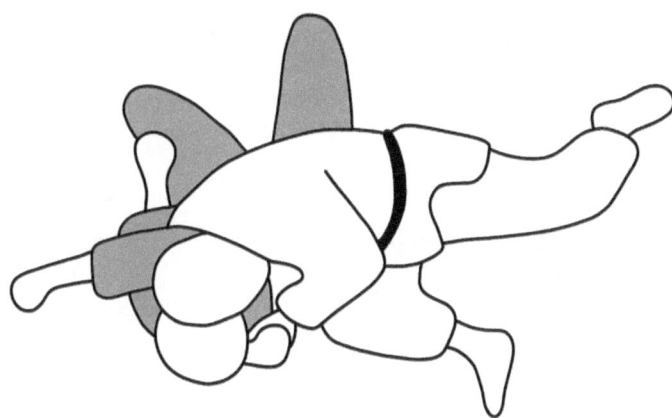

Description: Tori lies on their right side, while uke is on their back. Tori's right arm is wrapped over and around uke's neck. Uke's right arm is trapped by tori's head, pressed strongly against the upper arm. Tori's hands are joined behind uke's head. Tori's right leg is forward, left leg back. Tori tightens the arm grip and pushes their weight into uke's right arm and shoulder, lifting the shoulder off the ground and compressing uke's airway if possible by driving uke's right arm across the neck.

Common problems: Tori must establish a strong ground-line between their left foot and their own right shoulder, pressing hard against uke's arm with their head. This allows tori's body weight to reinforce the hold. Simply locking the hands together and squeezing is much less effective.

Defensive uses: This is an extremely uncomfortable hold-down technique if executed properly. It is painful, and makes breathing difficult for uke. If you are completely sure that nobody is going to intervene to assist your opponent, and you need to hold them in position for a time, *kata gatame* is useful.

Basic escapes: If you are trapped in *kata gatame*, you may try to turn your body, lifting the left shoulder and hopefully lowering the right. With your left hand, brace into the crook of your right arm at the bicep and lever your right arm downwards strongly against your opponent's right shoulder/upper arm. At the same time, bring your feet up under you and 'walk' yourself upwards, in the opposite direction to the downwards pressure of your arm. This should open enough space for you to try a quick, violent roll to the right, slipping under your opponent's top arm. To assist, slide your left hand down to your opponent's right elbow, keeping open the space you made earlier with continued pressure from your right elbow. As you attempt the roll, grab the opponent's right elbow with your left hand and push it up over your head as you roll away.

You may also try to bend your right elbow to bring your hand and wrist between your head and your opponent's head. Once that is done, bring your feet up close to your hips and bridge, pushing up with your hips and rolling towards your right shoulder. With your right hand in the position described, you may be able to make enough space to roll out altogether.

Basic changes and variations: If tori can control uke's right arm well enough, it is possible to encircle uke's head with their own right arm and trap the hand, allowing the choking element of the hold-down to be greatly intensified. If uke should free their right arm, tori can transition quickly to *mune gatame*, or *yoko shiho gatame*, or even *tate shiho gatame*.

Chest hold – *Mune gatame*

Description: Uke is on their back. Tori lies across uke's upper body at right angles, directing weight onto uke's chest. Tori's left arm passes under uke's left arm and takes a strong grip on the belt or jacket. Tori's right arm passes under uke's left from the opposite direction. Tori may brace with wide feet, or simply sprawl. Tori's head should be down, tucked into uke's shoulder as tori works to maintain control over the left arm. Uke's right arm is partially trapped below tori's body.

Common problems: *Mune gatame* is not a particularly strong hold down. It is difficult to apply any real discomfort to uke, or maintain control over uke's lower body in particular. It's mostly an intermediate position from which tori may try to take an arm lock, or shift to a stronger hold such as *kami shiho gatame* or *yoko shiho gatame*.

Defensive uses: In actual conflict, this isn't a position you would want to keep. You don't have enough control over uke, and no real means of inflicting pain or damage. You might transition through *mune gatame* as needed, but maintaining it takes more energy and concentration than it's worth.

Basic escapes: Bridge the hips strongly, then twist or roll.

Basic changes and variations: If uke lets their left arm get too far out from the body, tori is in a position to attempt a number of armlocks. It is also easy to transition from *mune gatame* into *yoko shiho gatame*, *kami shiho gatame*, or *tate shiho gatame*.

Side four-quarters hold — *Yoko shiho gatame*

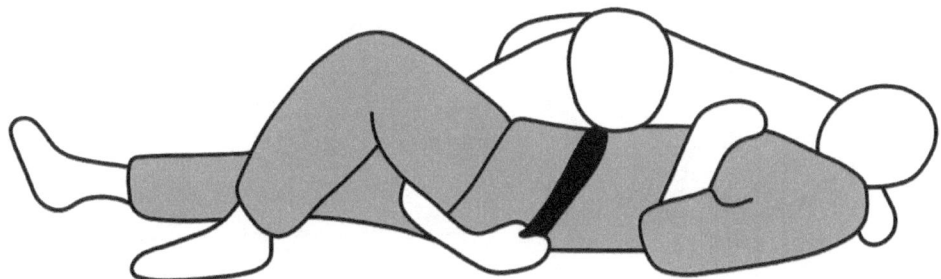

Description: Uke lies on their back. Tori lies at ninety degrees across uke, chest firmly pressed to uke's diaphragm region. Tori's left arm passes under uke's neck and around as far as possible to grab a hold on the gi. Tori's right arm passes between uke's legs, under uke's left thigh, and takes a strong grip on the belt or gi. Tori should drive their weight into uke's diaphragm, and squeeze tightly with both arms to force uke's head uncomfortably up and forward onto their chest. Tori's knees should be bent and splayed to keep the hips low, and tori should try to ensure that uke's right arm passes behind or over tori's back.

Common problems: If tori doesn't bring their knees up and splay them correctly uke may have enough room to roll inwards and escape the grip. If tori's right-hand grip isn't strong enough, uke may be able to straighten the right leg and compromise tori's hold.

Defensive value: Limited. This is a sporting hold. Uke has easy access to tori's head and face with the left hand, and tori has at best limited control over uke's right arm and hand.

Basic escapes: Uke can reach with their left hand over tori's left shoulder to seize tori's belt. If uke then slides their right hand under uke's left thigh and brings it up to immobilise the thigh it is reasonably easy to roll tori across uke's body to the left, and escape. Uke may also use the left arm against the side of tori's head to push it down, and attempt to trap it with the left leg.

Basic changes and variations: It is reasonably easy to transition from *yoko shiho gatame* into *tate shiho gatame* or *kami shiho gatame*. If uke straightens their leg and breaks the belt grip, tori can grab the leg of uke's gi and pin the leg to the mat, changing the hold to *kuzure yoko shiho gatame*.

Upper four quarters hold – *Kami shiho gatame*

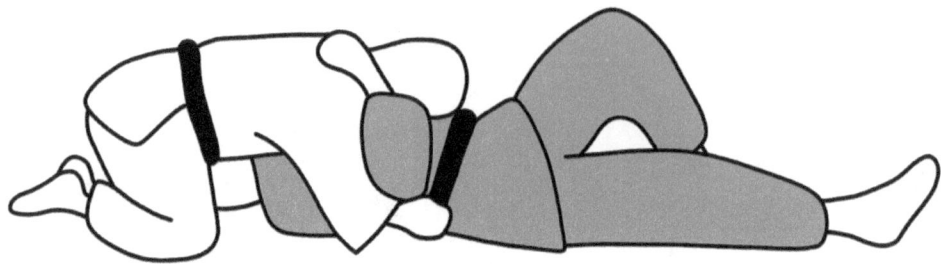

Description: Uke lies on their back. Tori lies over uke parallel, feet pointing the opposite direction. Tori threads both arms under uke's upper arms, strongly grasping uke's belt to trap uke's arms against uke's body. Tori lies heavily in close contact with uke, forcing uke to turn their face to one side in order to breathe. Whichever way uke turns their head, tori ensures that they draw up their knee on that side, at the very least as uke can otherwise attempt to roll in whatever direction they are facing.

Common problems: Tori must keep their head down and keep their weight firmly centred on uke. It is crucial to draw up the knee on the side that uke faces. Drawing up both knees may be better – but may also raise tori's hips too high for control. It is important that tori's bodyweight can be used to control uke's head.

Defensive value: Moderate. The hold-down is dependent on the belt grip, but that can often be improvised. Both uke's arms are reasonably controlled, but uke still has access to tori's face, hair and head. Biting isn't really a problem unless uke is willing to give up access to air in order to turn and bite. *Kami shiho gatame* is a strong position which offers a lot of possibilities.

Basic escapes: Drive with both hands, pushing up against tori's collar (neck, throat, face – whatever is legal or appropriate) The goal is to force tori to lift their head and upper body, allowing you to shift your hips and roll sharply to escape. You can also try to bridge your hips and walk your body quickly around, attempting to change the angle between you and tori until you have leverage enough to roll tori over.

Basic changes and variations: If uke manages to free an arm from being pinned to their side, tori can wrap over that arm to trap it, and change their body angle to get to *kuzure kami shiho gatame*. Tori may also respond to an arm escape with *ushiro kesa gatame*.

Upper four quarters hold – *Tate shiho gatame*

Description: Uke lies on their back. Tori lies atop uke, legs outside uke's. Tori's feet tuck under uke's thighs into the backs of the knees to trap the legs (called "grapevining" in wrestling.) Tori's head presses hard against uke's upper right arm and elbow to force it against and across uke's neck, while tori's right arm circle's uke's head and neck, passing underneath to join tori's left hand.

Common problems: If tori keeps their weight and position low on uke's body without properly grapevining, uke can bridge to throw tori off.

Defensive value: High. This position is very similar to the 'top mount' position of Brazilian jiu jitsu. It offers tori a great deal of control over uke's movement and even their breathing. If tori shifts their hips to ride high on uke's chest (splaying legs and knees to prevent easy rolling) it becomes difficult for uke to bridge and escape, and tori has opportunities either to strike at uke's head or try for armlocks or chokes. It is also easy for tori to disengage quickly if needed.

Basic escapes: If tori's weight is low on uke and tori has not successfully controlled uke's legs, uke can bridge suddenly and roll out. If uke has one arm free, they can 'frame' (join hands with the trapped arm) and used the combined strength of the arms to push against tori's collarbone, moving them lower so that uke can bridge and roll to escape.

Basic changes and variations: Tori can shift their hips farther up the body to look for striking options. Tori can dismount the legs and lower body, pivoting into *kata gatame*. Tori can also look for choking and strangling options easily from here.

Reverse scarf hold – *Ushiro kesa gatame*

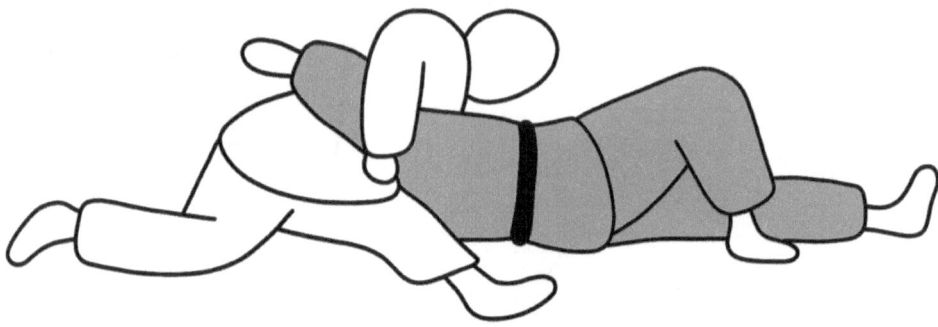

Description: Uke lies on their back. Tori leans across uke from over uke's right shoulder. Tori's right arm traps uke's right arm around tori's body, pinning strongly behind uke's right elbow. Tori's legs are splayed wide, and tori leans deeply over uke's body to apply weight to uke's torso. Tori's left hand may grip uke's belt, and their left elbow sits against uke's left arm, keeping it trapped back behind tori.

Common problems: If tori doesn't lean deep to apply weight, uke may be able to roll out to their right. If tori's legs aren't set correctly, uke may be able to roll tori across their body.

Defensive value: Moderate to low. Tori's control over uke is comparitively low, and uke's relatively free left arm represents a real danger.

Basic escapes: Uke grips tori's belt with the left hand, bridges strongly to make space, and rolls tori across to uke's left.

Basic changes and variations: Tori can slip back and across into *kuzure kami shiho gatame*, or roll forward to try for *yoko shiho gatame*.

Closed guard – *Do osae*

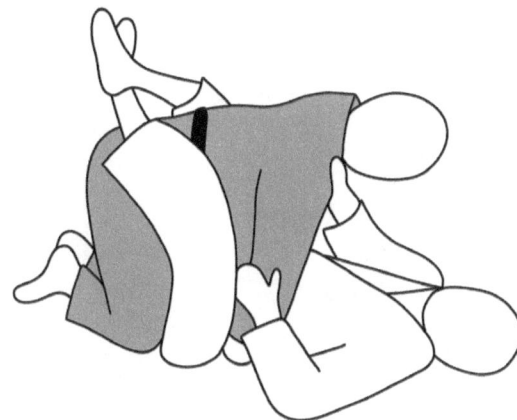

Description: Tori lies on their back. Uke is above and facing them, usually kneeling. Tori's legs are wrapped around uke's torso above the hips, crossed and locked at the ankles. Tori uses leg strength to keep uke close and control uke's movement. If possible, tori takes a controlling grip on uke's head, neck, or upper body to bring uke down and limit their movement.

Common problems: Tori must not simply lock their legs around uke's hips – the leg closure must be higher on the torso for safety and control. Tori should keep the grip tight, holding uke as closely as possible to prevent escape or other counter-attack.

Defensive value: High. This position was popularized by the BJJ movement, notably the Gracie school. It represents one end of a spectrum, the other being the 'open guard' where tori, on the ground, uses their open legs to control and counterattack an aggressor. In the closed guard, tori's most powerful muscles (in the legs) are available to lock onto uke's centre of gravity, providing considerable control over uke's movements. There are many fighting options from this position – BJJ has become synonymous with fighting on the ground, and this position is a mainstay of the system. Used correctly, it can help even a smaller (but trained) person resist a much larger untrained opponent.

Basic escapes: Uke can drive down into tori's inner thigh with bodyweight behind and elbow to open the guard through simple pain. Once the leg drops away, uke can very quickly throw tori's opposite leg up and over uke's head, allowing them to get past the guard.

Basic changes and variations: Tori can bring back a foot and push against uke's knee to off balance uke, allowing tori to roll uke into the bottom position to establish a top mount, or *tate shiho gatame*. Tori can trap one of uke's arms, and cast their opposite leg over uke's other shoulder to attempt a triangle choke.

Rear mount

Description: Tori lies behind uke. (Rear mount can be done from above or below.) Tori's legs pass around uke's torso, with tori's feet inside uke's thighs. Tori controls uke's upper body and head by encircling the head with one arm, and locking onto the other arm which slides under uke's opposite arm.

Common problems: If tori doesn't establish control over uke's head quickly enough, uke can slip the leg hold in a variety of ways. Tori must press close to uke, keeping their head down.

Defensive value: Very high. This is another powerful technique popularised by Brazilian Jujitsu. In a one-on-one situation, this position is extremely useful. It permits control over uke's movement, keeps tori out of the range of uke's weapons, and allows tori to attack with a variety of choking and locking techniques including the devastating *hadaka jime* (rear naked choke.)

Basic escapes: If tori is careless about the upper body control, uke can swiftly grab tori's feet with both hands, and use the grip as a 'lever point' to drive their elbows forcefully into uke's calves where the muscle meets the shinbone. This is extremely painful, and will cause most opponents – particularly untrained opponents – to open their legs and escape.

However if tori has established the position well, the best uke can do is get a hand inside tori's arms to prevent the choke, and then work towards freeing up their legs or head. Once this position is well established by a trained fighter, it is very difficult to escape.

Basic changes and variations: From here, tori can seek a range of strangles with or without the jacket. Tori can also look for arm and shoulder locks as uke attempts to free themself.

Anatomy and vulnerable points

Head, neck, and throat 152
Torso 154
Arms and hands 155
Legs and feet 156

Making your technique count

My first instructor, Shihan Mark Haseman, had a party trick that he would use when we were training security workers back in the day. These were usually big, powerful men; weightlifters and bodybuilders with tremendous strength and an air of confidence rooted in the belief that no matter what came in front of them, they were physically strong enough to deal with it. It's difficult to teach alternative ways of handling potentially violent situations to a man who believes his fists can answer every question. Mark's method of opening their eyes was, very simply, to demonstrate that their fists weren't as all-powerful as they thought.

He would pick one from each new group of trainees. Sometimes it would be the largest. Sometimes the loudest. He would compliment them on their strength and power, and he was genuine when he did it. They usually didn't know what to say. They weren't mentally prepared for compliments. They were even less prepared for what came next.

Mark would invite them to punch him in the belly.

It helps if you picture it: a man in his mid to late forties, of average height, carrying a touch more weight than perhaps he should, gently challenging a human behemoth with muscles in places where most people don't even have places to slug him in the gut with everything they had. Invariably, it took a good two to five minutes of quiet persuasion before the muscle-man finally agreed to take the shot – but in the end, they always agreed.

Mark's face would go blank. He'd stare off into the middle distance, and he'd nod. Then the big man, face still wary with disbelief, would step up and throw some kind of punch at Mark's midriff. These were not small men. I was there as an assistant to help out with the training (and to improve my own skills) and some of these men had arms the size of my thighs.

Sometimes they even managed to make Mark take a half-step back. Occasionally there was a soft grunt. Then he would nod, and clap the astonished muscleman on the shoulder, and compliment him on the power of his punch, and we'd go on with the lesson.

How did it work?

Mark knew damned well the men we were training didn't understand how to bring the full power of their bodies to bear on a punch. He also knew where the vulnerable places on his own body were, and he was careful to direct the punches elsewhere. Honestly? If you've got half-decent abdominal muscles and a sense of timing, this stunt is no big deal at all. I mean, yeah, it will leave a good bruise. But if you breathe out and tighten your muscles at the right moment, and maybe lean into the punch a little – well, first you'll make his fist hit you before he actually reaches full power. And second, you'll engage some of the strongest muscles in your body to lock down and absorb the impact. It looks like magic, but really, it's just a matter of knowing your own anatomy.

If you don't know where to hit someone, much of the power of your punches is simply wasted. Ju jutsu isn't about using brute strength to overcome somebody else. It's about using minimal energy, minimal force to create maximum effect. One way to maximise the effect of your techniques is to target vulnerable parts of your opponent's anatomy. There are quite a lot of those, and you need to know how to attack them properly to get the best effect. To cover the topic, we will divide the body into different sections and discuss the vital points of each separately.

Please note: in keeping with the rest of the book, this is not a comprehensive list of vital points. It's an introductory, basic guide to those most frequently referenced in basic training. There are many others.

Also note: I've made no mention of acupuncture points or 'meridians'. I know what hurts when I hit it. If you want someone who knows Deadly Death Touch Fu, you need another book entirely.

Head, neck, and throat

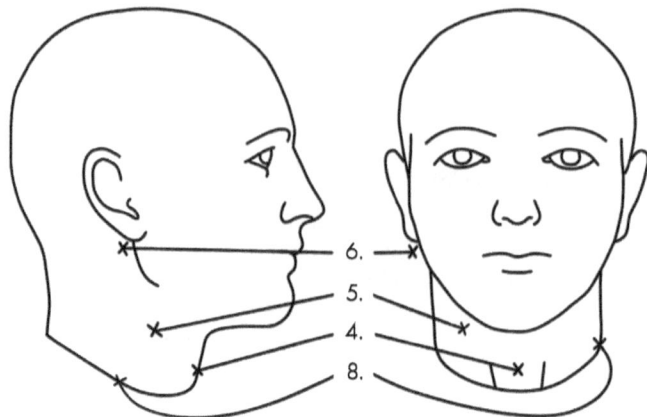

1. Eyes: Extremely sensitive, easily damaged. Direct pressure causes intense pain. Protected by bony brow ridge, and most people have very deep-seated protective reflexes with regard to their eyes. Please note – while the pain from being poked in the eye is pretty nasty, it's not 'game over' by any means. And if somebody with a little skill in judo, ju jutsu, sambo, wrestling or a similar grappling game gets their hands on you, they really don't need their vision to take you apart.
2. Ears: The external ear is sensitive to direct pressure and sharp impacts, which cause great pain. Hollowing the palm and 'clapping' over the ear opening can cause a painful, disorienting pressure wave to attack the eardrum. The external ear also makes an excellent hand grip for dragging your opponent's head around, but be careful: they're only attached by a bit of skin.
3. Nose: No. You can't kill someone by breaking their nose and driving the bones into their brain, okay? Forget that. It's dumb. But noses are very sensitive structures. A sharp slap to the nose hurts like hell and makes the eyes water. Driving pressure up into the septum (the bit that separates the nostrils) is extremely painful and can be used to control your opponent's head. Breaking the nose takes relatively little force, and usually results in a lot of blood, which is probably not what you're after.
4. Windpipe (trachea): I'm including the voicebox (larynx) here. Easily found semi-rigid body at front of neck. Reinforced with bands of cartilage, the windpipe takes air down to the lungs. It is defended by nerves which make it sensitive to pressure, so it can be grabbed and squeezed for pain control. A strong strike to the windpipe may collapse it, resulting in death by choking/asphyxiation. Striking to the neck and throat should always be a last resort.
5. Carotid Artery: Found at the side of the neck between the sternocleidomastoid muscle and the windpipe. Supplies blood to the brain. Protected by nerves making it very sensitive to pressure. Hook your fingers in front of the SCM muscle to get a grip that drives your fingertips into the carotid artery to control the movement of your opponent's head. Sufficient pressure to the carotid will reduce blood flow to the brain, leading to unconsciousness.
6. Facial Nerve: The stem of the facial nerve is found behind the point of the jawbone, just below and in front of the earlobe. Direct pressure here is excruciating to most people, allowing for head control. A pinpoint strike is difficult to achieve, but the pain is explosive and devastating.
7. Jaw hinge: The jawbone (mandible) is attached to the skull by a hinge joint which lets the jaw move up and down, for chewing. It isn't designed to go sideways. A sharp strike to the side of the mandible can badly damage or dislocate the jaw hinge/hinges. This is painful and disorienting.
8. Carotid Body/Carotid Sinus: These two are close enough together to treat them as one. The carotid body is a nerve cluster, highly sensitive to pressure. The carotid sinus includes pressure receptors

which register blood pressure to the brain. A sharp and accurate strike to the carotid sinus can potentially produce a 'pressure spike' which will lead the carotid sinus to signal for a sharp drop in blood pressure, resulting in almost immediate fainting (syncope). This is the origin of the legendary "karate neck chop" seen in so many spy films. It is also a lot harder to pull off in real life, and has many potentially dangerous side effects. *Striking to the neck and throat should always be a last resort.*

9. Underside of jaw: Under the edge of the jawbone (mandible) there are a range of delicate, sensitive structures including glands, ganglia, and nerves. Direct pressure underneath the jaw causes great pain, and the jaw structure makes an excellent gripping 'handle' to let the fingers curl under and wreak havoc.

10. Chin: A direct strike to the chin can transmit the force of the strike back through the jawbone to the skull, and produce a 'knockout'. This is "the button" that boxers hope to hit. You'll note that knockout strikes are rarely seen, which should tell you how difficult it really is to achieve this end. Further, a strike with closed fist to the jawbone risks your own finger bones. If you miss and hit the mouth and teeth you're going to get badly cut, and without medical treatment you will almost certainly get a dangerous bacterial infection.

11. Mouth: The lips are sensitive, sure. But the teeth are right behind the lips. Hitting people in the mouth risks damage to your hands, and does very little to discourage them from hitting you back. Leave the mouth alone. It's a poor target.

Torso

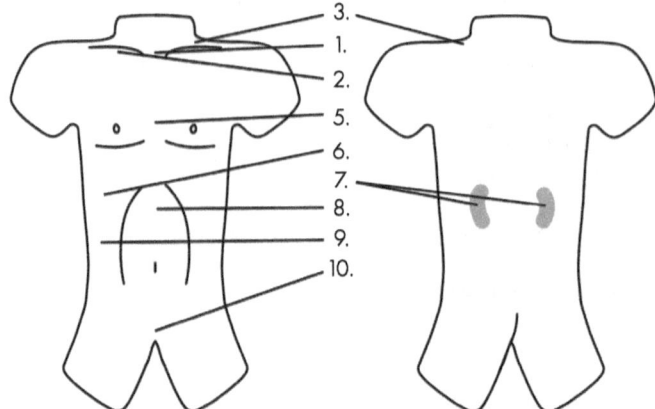

1. Jugular Notch: Where the two collarbones come together at the base of the throat, just above the breastbone. Drive fingers inward to attack the windpipe and cause pain. Hook the fingers and drive over and down to attack both windpipe AND the nerves around the subclavian artery for extra bonus points.
2. Collarbone (clavicle): Relatively vulnerable to a good, solid downward strike. Breaking the collarbone tends to make operating the arm on that side difficult, as well as being quite painful.
3. Brachial Plexus (above collarbone): A very large bundle of nerves travels through this region. Attack with direct strikes, or by driving your fingers into the area above the collarbone to cause tremendous pain.
4. Armpit: The axillary nerve runs down through here. You get different effects depending on how and where you strike. Drive your fingers deep and up into the armpit to strike the nerve cluster, potentially causing temporary paralysis to the arm – and enormous pain. Drive deep into the armpit against the rib cage to cause sickening pain and impaired breathing.
5. Heart: Well protected by ribs and musculature, but a solid, powerful blow can hit the 'pacemaker' nerves, causing 'commotio cordis' – basically, sending the heart into a fatal spasm. (This is a noted injury from baseball, for example, when the ball hits the chest hard and accurately.) This is unlikely to happen as the heart has to be at just the right point in its rhythm when the impact occurs... but it's very lethal very quickly. Probably not a great idea to be punching people in the heart unless you really, really don't like them and maybe you're keen on a stretch in prison.
6. Liver: Right hand side, about midway down. Much of the liver is protected by the strong ribcage, but the lower portion is vulnerable to a good, strong strike to that area. Even in professional cage fighting, a shot to the liver is regarded as something to fear. The pain is intense and disabling. If you can get in a good strike to your opponent's liver, you can probably drop the mike and walk away.
7. Kidneys: These organs are reasonably well protected, but if you can target them with an accurate strike the pain is intense and disabling. Be careful – a ruptured kidney will cause shock and death in short order.
8. Solar plexus: There's actually a huge nerve cluster here, with several plexuses affecting different organs. It's deep, protected by the abdominal muscles – but if you strike there powerfully when your opponent is relaxed (breathing in) you will cause disabling pain, as well as great difficulty in breathing.
9. Floating ribs: The lowest couple of ribs on either side don't connect directly to the sternum, and are called 'false' or 'floating' ribs. They are relatively vulnerable to striking attacks. They hurt like hell when they get hit, and make breathing quite a challenge when they're broken.
10. Groin: There's just an acre of vulnerable stuff here. And don't let anyone fool you – women hate being crotch-kicked every bit as much as men do. Target the centreline in either sex to cause intense, disabling pain. Note that in men, at least, this pain can 'hold off' for four to six seconds, so don't expect your opponent to just drop like a stone. Note also that adults have very strong protective reflexes for this area, so it isn't the great target that many people believe it to be.

Arms and Hands

1. Shoulder Joint: Can be locked up for structural control, pain compliance, or for dislocation. Dislocation effectively makes the arm stop working. May also stop the opponent due to pain.
2. Point of the shoulder: Hook your fingers in from behind and drive into the bony process at the front to cause pain by pushing into nerves in front of the bone. Useful for straightening someone up if you're applying a rear arm entanglement.
3. Radial nerve (upper arm): On the inside of the arm near the armpit. Strike hard in that area to cause intense pain and temporary paralysis of the arm. Grip the humerus and curl your fingers over to drive into the nerve for pain compliance.
4. Elbow: Basic hinge joint vulnerable to hyperextension. Lock it up for structural control and pain compliance, or over-extend it to tear the joint apart and destroy arm function.
5. Radial nerve (lower arm): Strike sharply to the upper inside of the radius (the bone that runs from elbow to thumb) to hit the radial nerve. Makes an effective target for a strong knife-hand block. If you hit it accurately, you may cause the hand to open involuntarily, and make it useless for a short period.
6. Wrist: Hinge joint. Not so much leverage available as at the elbow – difficult to destroy with hyperextension, but hyperflexion (folding the wrist down) can do serious damage. Joint locks for structural control and pain compliance, or tear the joint apart to make the hand useless.
7. Hands/Fingers: Fingers can be locked up early in the conflict, but once the adrenaline is flowing many fighters will simply not notice broken or dislocated fingers. However, the bundle of small bones all together there is a useful target. It's an ugly thing to suggest, but stamping on the hand of a downed opponent (assuming the conflict is ongoing and you remain in danger) is an effective way of putting that particular weapon out of the fight.

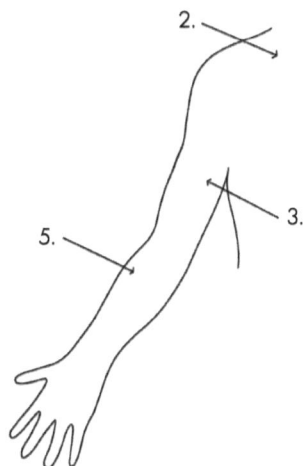

Legs and Feet

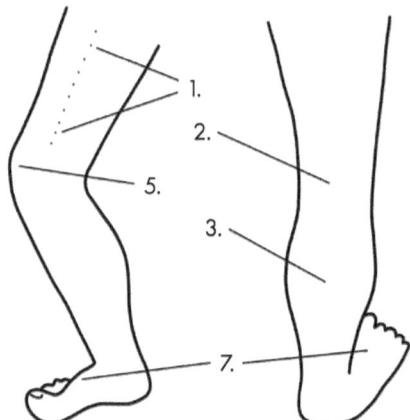

1. Femoral Nerve – runs down the inside of the thigh. Hit it hard to cause tremendous pain and collapse the leg.
2. Popliteal Nerve – part of a nerve cluster directly behind the knee. Drive in with fingers to cause pain compliance. Strike hard and accurately to collapse the leg and cause temporary partial paralysis of the limb.
3. Tibial Nerve – Strike hard between the two horns of the calf muscle to cause stunning pain and temporary partial paralysis of the lower leg and foot.
4. Knee: Hinge joint. May be hyperextended with a kneebar, but this takes a good deal of strength and technique. If the knee is straight, a strong kick through the front or side may do enough structural damage to pull the joint apart and collapse the leg.
5. Kneecap (patella): Sesamoid bone on the front of the kneejoint. Sesamoid bones are 'floating' bones that don't really contribute to the structural integrity of the skeleton proper... but if you kick a kneecap accurately and sharply from the side, you can pop it round to the back of the leg. And when that happens, the leg no longer bends – and it hurts like hell.
6. Ankle: Can be joint-locked and damaged, but it's a strong joint and it's hard to isolate it without getting your head kicked off by the other foot. A strong, stomping kick from the front or side can do damage.
7. Instep: That's the top of the foot, full of small, crunchy bones. Stomp it to distract, and to make it hard for your opponent to stand or pursue you. Toes can be stomped too.

The difference between learning the techniques and learning the art of Ju Jutsu

You've reached the end of the technical content in this book. Suppose you and a buddy took this book, found yourself a nice, quiet spot with a decent mat, and worked hard at it together. If I've written clearly enough, you could just about learn all the techniques in the book, in time. So – that would be learning ju jutsu, right?

No. *Not even close.*

First of all, this is a handbook of *basic* techniques. I've left out many more that I know because they're not part of what I've seen as the commonplace repertoire across a range of different ju jutsu systems and schools. But more than that: every single instructor I've ever met also had a bunch of techniques I don't know. In fact, a lot of *students* from other styles and systems know techniques I don't know. And then there are variations on the techniques, and variations on the variations. And of course, many ju jutsu systems incorporate a lot of weapons work as well. Ju jutsu is one damn' big art.

Beyond that, there are the different applications of the techniques – from gentle, quick escapes out of simple grabs up to devastating counters to dangerous multiple-attacker scenarios. The individual techniques are really just simple building blocks. Knowing how to do them is one thing. Knowing how they are applied is entirely another, and if I tried to write a book on that topic I couldn't cover it in a thousand pages.

But even if I covered the applications of the techniques and you practiced those too, you still wouldn't have learned ju jutsu. Underneath the techniques and the applications there lies the real art: the deep principles which make the techniques function. There are principles of biomechanics and movement. Principles of distance and angle. Principles of energy – its use and redirection. There are principles of the psychology of conflict. Principles of control and limitation. Each effective technique works because it follows and fulfils these deeper principles, and the real art of ju jutsu comes from internalizing these principles, understanding them without thought so you can move from technique to technique as the situation demands.

You don't get that from a book. You don't even get it from all the books, or the videos, or the practice patterns. You get it from an instructor who has at least some of that understanding, and you acquire it for yourself by long, hard practice with a decent range of training partners who are prepared to commit themselves just as fully. You have to practice getting the techniques right. Then you have to practice applying the techniques against pre-set attacks. Then you have to apply the techniques against unpredictable attacks. Then you need to do more of the same, but with resistant opponents who will try to fight back against you. And after every session, every new batch of bruises and strained muscles, you need to review what you did right and wrong, think it through, and get ready to try it again.

Technically, ju jutsu is 'jutsu', not '–do'. Technically, it's just a 'method' or a 'system', not a Way or a Path, something that's meant to enlighten and improve you spiritually. After more than thirty years around martial arts, I don't really know what that means any more. What I do know: if you put in the time and the effort required to get a decent grip on the art of ju jutsu, you will learn an enormous amount about yourself, and you will grow immeasurably. The art will change you even as you adapt it to yourself. You'll be more confident, more relaxed, stronger, fitter... You'll be part of a very special community of like-minded people, and a piece of a strong, enduring tradition that spans continents and centuries.

Is it worth the effort, in the end?

That's up to you. You get out of it what you put in. It's been part of my life over thirty years now. I have no intention of stopping this side of the grave.

Further reading

I will repeat for clarity: you can't learn ju jutsu from reading. But you can learn a great deal *about* ju jutsu, about martial arts, and about self-defense from reading. A student who reads carefully and thinks about what they discover will find in the right books much that will help them understand and refine their own practice. Here are some recommendations:

Sun Tzu – "Art of War" written thousands of years ago in China, this very small volume (which can be found free on the Internet if you so desire) is quick, simple and to the point. Yet there's also subtlety and depth to the work. It was written to explain basic principles of successfully waging war in the Bronze and early Iron age – but the clarity, simplicity and honesty of the book has made it a military classic which is still required reading. Even though it was intended for armies and kingdoms, the ideas are clear and simple and much of the work applies very nicely to principles of personal conflict and self defense.

Miyamoto Musashi's – "Book of Five Rings," Musashi was a samurai of the early Edo period in Japan. He is revered as the greatest swordsman of his age – and unquestionably one of the greatest in history – but his practice of martial arts led him to become much more. His book offers insight into the methods, philosophy, and mindset which allowed him to prevail in over sixty duels, some of which were against pre-eminent warriors and swordsmen of the era. It is also an intriguing window into the discipline and the "way" of the Samurai, and their inextricable association with the swords they carried.

Rory Miller – "Meditations on Violence," "Preparing for Violence": Miller is a modern figure, an American police officer with a long history in martial arts. Miller writes with remarkable clarity on his chosen topics, and in so doing deconstructs many of the prevailing myths around the practice and study of martial arts. The books are short and easily consumed. They should be considered required reading not just for martial arts students, but for anyone who recognizes the possibility that violence may crop up in their lives.

Mark Haseman – "Tohkon Ryu Ju Jitsu": Most of the available books on ju jutsu are focused on particular schools, styles or systems. I have selected this one for attention for several reasons. First, Shihan Haseman was my own first instructor in ju jutsu, and the decades have not diminished my respect for his clear, no-nonsense approach. But more importantly, the book dives deep into territory that most style- or system-based texts avoid. Haseman explicitly lays out deeper principles and ideas, offering not so much technique as an understanding of how and when and why techniques apply – and just as importantly, do not apply. An excellent insight into a modern, highly relevant ju jutsu system.

Also, Mark's illustrations are much, much nicer than mine.

Afterword

This turned out to be a bigger job of work than I anticipated, but it was fun nevertheless. In researching through books and websites for comparisons on technique, I discovered many minor ideas and details which were new to me, some of which I have decided to keep in my own practice. That's ju jutsu, after all: adapting, learning and growing.

That is a point I really can't make clear enough. While there are traditional 'koryu' styles of ju jutsu which take pride in holding to methods that haven't altered in centuries, that isn't how the art began. Ju jutsu started – as near as we can tell from historic records – as a collection of techniques shared between men who had a difficult, violent job to fulfill. Remember: the samurai were soldiers; battlefield fighters. It wasn't a hobby or a side interest to them. The difference between a technique that worked and a technique that was too soft or too complicated or too slow was literally the difference between life and death. Bad techniques died out, while good techniques were shared or stolen, refined and expanded.

The same process is going on even now. Sure, modern soldiers have more efficient ways of killing each other, but in Krav Maga and the MCMAP (US Marine combatives programme) you can still see techniques that the samurai would have recognized in centuries long gone. And in gyms and dojos and fighting rings and cages around the world, the same thing is happening.

It's my belief that ju jutsu practitioners need to embrace change, not fear it. After all, there are many different ways and reasons to practice the art. Not everyone wants to fight in a cage – and successful cage-fighting techniques aren't particularly well suited to breaking up a drunken hair-pulling match between two college-age women. And neither of those two concepts sit well with the precision and performance of a classic historical ju jutsu practice. Rather than claiming superiority for one style over another, we need to ask ourselves what we want to practice ju jutsu *for*, and then pursue the techniques and ideas which best let us do exactly that.

This book will not teach you ju jutsu. We've been over that: you need an instructor, a place to practice, and people to train with. No amount of books and videos will ever change that. This book doesn't even come close to laying out the range of techniques available to the art. It's just a simple helper, an aid to memory that can assist a student with names and movements and very basic concepts. If you really want to learn, go find a class and an instructor.

Not tomorrow. *Right now.*

See you on the mat!

Basic Terms and Vocabulary

arigato – thank you
ashi – leg, foot
ate – hit, strike
atemi waza – striking technique
barai/harai – sweep
bo – staff for fighting or walking
chudan – halfway up (body level)
do – 'Way', spiritual discipline
dojo – 'hall of the Way'; training hall
empi/enpi – elbow strike
eri – collar
gaeshi/kaeshi – counter
gake – hook
garami – entangle, wrap
gatame – lock, hold
gedan – downward, below (low level)
geri/keri – kick
gi – uniform
go – five
goshi/koshi – hip
goshin jutsu – self defence
guruma – wheel
gyaku – reverse
hachi – eight, eighth. Sometimes the 'uppermost eighth' of the body: the head
hadaka – bare, naked
haito – ridge hand
hajime – begin
hanbo – 1 metre fighting stick
hane – jump, spring, leap
hara – belly
hidari – left
hiji – elbow
hiki – pull
hiki te – pulling hand
hineri – twist, spin
hishigi – crush
hiza – knee
ichi – one
idori – seated, kneeling
irimi – entering, stepping in
jime/shime – strangle, choke
jo – short staff (waist heigh staff)
jodan – high, raised (upper level)
ju – soft, flexible, yielding, adaptable
judo – 'Gentle Way', sport/art
juji – cross, crossed
ju jutsu – flexible/adaptable/gentle method

jutsu – art, system, method
kake – point where a throw takes effect
kansetsu – joints
kata (1) – shoulder
kata (2) – martial training pattern
kesa – scarf, stole
kiai – spirit shout, martial shout
ko – small, minor, lesser
kote – forearm
kubi – neck, neckband
kuzure – break, broken
kyu – nine, ninth
mae – forward, front
mate – stop, wait
migi – right
mikazuki – crescent moon
morote – two handed, two hands
mune – chest
nage – throw
nage waza – throwing techniques
nami – common, ordinary, usual
ne – lying down
ni – two, second
nuki te – spear hand
o – large, great, major
obi – belt
okuri – sliding
osaekomu – to hold down
osaekomi waza – pinning techniques
otoshi – drop
randori – free grappling practice
rei – respect (verbal signal to bow)
renshu – practice
ritsurei – standing bow
roku – six, sixtth
ryu – school
san – three, third
seiken – forefist
seiza – kneeling position
sensei – instructor, teacher
seoi – on the back
seoi nage – shoulder throw
shi – four, fourth
shichi – seven, seventh
shihan – master, senior teacher
shime waza – strangling/choking techniques
shotei – palm heel
shuto – knife hand

160 *Launz Burch*

sode – sleeve
soto – outer, outside
sukui – scooping
sumi – corner, angle
sutemi waza – sacrifice techniques
tachi – stand, stance
tai – body
tambo – forearm-length fighting stick
tani – valley
tanto – dagger
tatami – mat
tate – divide vertically, split lengthwise; length
te – hand
te kubi – wrist
tobi – jump, fly
toho – sword peak palm
tokui waza – favoured or preferred techniques
tori – active partner, doer, thrower
uchi – inside, inner
uchikomi – 'fitting in', repetitive throwing
ude – arm, upper arm
uke – receive, receiver
ukemi – break fall
uki – float, floating
ura – to the rear
ushiro – back, behind
utsuri – change
wakare – separation, division
waki – armpit, flank
waza – techniques
yama – mountain
yoko – side
yon – four, fourth
yubi – finger
zarei – formal kneeling bow

NOTES

www.ingramcontent.com/pod-product-compliance
Lightning Source LLC
Chambersburg PA
CBHW030257010526
44107CB00053B/1747